THE PREACHING EVENT

Also by John Claypool:

Stages: The Art of Living the Expected
Tracks of a Fellow Struggler

LYMAN BEECHER LECTURES

THE
PREACHING
EVENT

JOHN R. CLAYPOOL

WORD BOOKS
PUBLISHER
4800 WEST WACO DRIVE
WACO, TEXAS
76703

THE PREACHING EVENT

ISBN 0-8499-0131-6
Library of Congress Catalog Card No.: 79-67669
Printed in the United States of America

To my son
Rowan
who shared with me
the days at Yale
and
added to their joy

Contents

Introduction

The material in the pages to follow was prepared and delivered at the Yale Divinity School
on February 13–15, 1979, as the Lyman Beecher
Lectures on Preaching. I learned much in reading some eighty-five of the one hundred and
seven presentations that preceded my own in
this august tradition. I also experienced something very profound on my own in the final
weeks of preparation. In fact, the experience was
so meaningful to me that I want to share it with
you as a preface to the lectures themselves.

No question in all the religious realm has
intrigued me more than this: "In the drama of
everyday events, what does God do and what

do we humans do?" I have found it impossible to arrive at any exact formula in answer to such a question, although I realize certain other folk have no such problem and speak definitively about this matter.

For example, many so-called conservatives come down hard on the side of divine preeminence in this area. God does practically everything and we humans do practically nothing in the drama of existence, according to them. "Let go and let God" is a familiar saying among folk of this persuasion. Their model of divine-human interaction is a complete emptying of self and a renunciation of all personal initiative and desires on the one hand, and the total absorption by God of personality on the other. "God is everything, I am nothing" becomes the ideal.

I once heard this position depicted in a very graphic image. It seems that an American Indian was converted to this form of Christianity and went back to the reservation to share his new-found faith. However, he seemed unable to get the message across in words, so he resorted to more tangible means. He found an earthworm and set it down in the middle of a circle of dried leaves. Then he set the leaves on fire, and the people watched as the worm instinctively recognized its danger and began to try to escape, turning first this way and then that. However, in every direction it was met with a wall of fire. Finally, realizing that the situation was hopeless, the worm crawled back to the center, as far as it could get from the heat, and visibly went limp, giving up the effort to escape altogether. At that point, the convert reached down and plucked the worm out of the flames and said, "This is what it means to be saved. When we abandon all efforts to do anything for ourselves, becoming absolutely immobile and helpless, that is when God becomes active, but not before."

This image sums up very well the thinking of those conservative groups who put the whole emphasis on the Godward side in the equation of history. "I can't, but He can," "God is everything, I am nothing" become their watchwords, and it follows logically that groups like this put little emphasis on education or social involvement in any form. They view the human role in the drama of history as largely passive, as being acted upon rather than acting. God is Subject and we are objects in this way of understanding the pattern of events.

But then there is also the polar opposite of this position. There are other Christians who place the emphasis heavily on human initiative and action. To be sure, God is not left out altogether.

He was present at the beginning—creating the world to operate according to certain principles—and he will be around at the end to give us a grade on our performances, but during the time in between, we humans are pretty much on our own. "The heavens belong to God," these folk are fond of saying, "the earth—it belongs to us; that is, what is done here depends largely on human ingenuity and goodness and courage." There is no such thing as divine intervention or miracle or rescue in this way of thinking. To expect such is regarded as infantile regression, wanting to stay a baby when in fact we have to grow up and take responsibility for ourselves and our actions and the earth and the world. This is the way more liberal denominations tend to approach the equation of history, and again it is not surprising that they have had a high commitment to education and political action and whatever comes of purely human initiatives. If the words "Let go and let God" epitomize the folk on the extreme right, the words of the great pioneer in social work, Jane Addams, epitomize the left: "If not now, when? If not you, who?" The heavens, remember, are where God works. The earth belongs to us, and everything depends on how well or how poorly we choose to act.

Now admittedly, I have stated these two positions in a most extreme way. They do, however, form the framework of American Christianity and all of its various denominational expressions. So the question remains: How are we to understand these activities of divinity and humanity in the events of history?

I repeat: I can find no satisfaction in either one of these more-or-less "exact" formulations. My own reading of Holy Scripture points to something more complex than either extreme—God as the sole Actor in history, or humans as abandoned orphans who have to fend for themselves. The picture that comes to me from history, all the way from Abraham to Jesus to the early church, is the image of a duet or even of a dance—where one Partner invites the other to participate in a shared adventure. And when there is positive response, something comes about that neither one of the two could have created by themselves.

For example, when Abraham was confronted initially by this mysterious desert God named Yahweh (Gen. 12), the following pattern emerged. Things were proposed for Abraham's future that he would never have considered if he had been left on his own—a land to call his own, descendants more numerous than the stars of the sky, a name that would be remembered throughout all of history, a way by which all the families of earth could bless themselves. I would have to call this direct intervention. It is not the action of some watchmakerlike God who creates a world, winds it up, and then goes off to leave it until at last it runs down. No, here is intervention in the midst of history, God calling an individual by his very own name and offering to make certain things possible that clearly would have been beyond the reach of this individual's natural powers. It was an invitation to share in a more-than-human enterprise. Yet notice closely that Abraham was not asked to go limp like that worm and have all this done to him passively. There was a role for him to play in this new "dance step," if I can call it that. In fact, what was asked of Abraham was utterly unheard of for that moment of history. He was to leave his clan and country, his familiar surroundings, and venture out toward a land that would be shown him as he made the journey. At a time before individualism had ever been thought of, this was quite a challenge, yet Abraham accepted— he joined the duet and stepped out on the floor to learn a new dance step. And this was the beginning of biblical religion—a religion not of God doing everything and human beings doing nothing, or of human beings doing everything and God doing nothing, but *a mystery of creative collaboration when the two become one and yet remain two at the same time,* neither one absorbing the other into themselves, but dancing, if you please, as only two can dance. I see this as the secret of authentic Christian experience and true religious creativity.

I perceive this most clearly in the life of Jesus of Nazareth. He was by no means "a limp leaf on a wet log," merely allowing himself to be an object before some overwhelming Subject. He acted with all the marks of true individuality. At the same time, again and again, he went out and prayed all night; he claimed that none of the extraordinary things he did were his own completely but were done in conjunction with the Father whose working enabled him to work and whose giving made it possible for him to give. That sense of two becoming one and yet remaining two characterizes all his days and nights. It has become my theoretical model for attempting to image the way Divinity and humanity interact.

This image ceased to be abstract theory and took on new meaning as I worked to prepare the Beecher Lectures. The gracious invitation to do this work came from Dean Colin Williams almost two years before the lectures were to be given, and from the moment of my acceptance, I began to think about the project and to gather material for it. It was at this point that I set for myself the goal of reading as many of the former Beecher lectures as possible, so as to get the feel of this stream into which I would step.

The matter of timing my preparation appropriately particularly concerned me. I have worked for twenty-five years as a parish minister and so am used to a close proximity of preparation and presentation. I once had to give the Annual Sermon at the Southern Baptist Convention, and they required that the manuscript be in by March although the convention was not until June. Such a time lapse was for me a negative thing—the material did not have the freshness I was used to in the week-to-week parish setting. Thus, I was anxious not to formulate the lectures so far ahead of time that they might become stale. At the same time, I did not want to wait so long as to become pressed and not able to do the crafting the way it should be done. Out of both of these concerns I blocked out the month of January—the lectures were scheduled for February 13–15—to give final form to material already gathered and mulled over extensively.

By the end of the second week of January, although I had worked diligently for several hours each day, I had gotten absolutely nowhere. Not one word had been set down on paper. To be honest with you, a sense of panic began to set in. I thought to myself: "Here I have had two years, and now I am about to make an absolute fool of myself!" All kinds of self-recrimination and anxieties swept over me. One afternoon in deep anguish I laid down my pencil and, in what might be called an "exercise in honesty," I took the whole situation straight to the Father. I openly acknowledged how locked and immobile I was at the point of creativity, and admitted the panic that was building up because of this. Please understand that I did not hear any audible voice or see any visual images. But after I had emptied myself before my Maker, the following impression came to me:

The people at Yale would like to renegotiate this contract. They would prefer that Jesus of Nazareth give these lectures, for across the years, the words that have really been significant have all emanated from him. However (and I smile now when I think about it), the impression came that Jesus had laryngitis at this time and would be unable to give the lectures himself.

Would I be willing to agree to work with him in the formulation of the material and then take them to New Haven and deliver them in his stead? If this were agreeable, it came to me that I would have to work very hard and be available to receive the material as he would give it. It would be like a telegraph operator sitting by a receiver set, ready to take down and decode the messages that come over. I was also made to feel that I must not be afraid or anxious anymore. He would take responsibility for getting the material together in time to give it. He was aware of the dates. He could be depended on. It was not up to me to worry, but simply to work in receiving and then go and deliver them as best I could.

This new contract "suited me to a T," given the impasse in which I found myself, and so I got out my journal and proceeded to write it out word for word—what he was to do and what I was to do. And all I can report to you is that from that day forward, things flowed with incredible creativity. I never worked as hard in my life as I did in the subsequent five weeks. The experience was not at all like the worm crawling to the middle of the circle and absolutely giving up. There was intense human effort on my part as I thought about ideas and words, evaluated them as best I could, wrote and rewrote. Yet I can testify that in the midst of all this I had the feeling I was working with Another. It was not as if I had been reduced to something impersonal and was being dictated to, but there was another Presence with me in the study upstairs at home, and the giving of the material itself in New Haven had the feel of a duet and not a solo.

This experience was not utterly new to me, because week after week I try both to preach and do my other work in this way. However, this was my most dramatic experience of the mystery of collaboration. It helps me understand what St. Paul meant in writing to the Corinthians when he spoke of the grace that enabled him to join the Christian community (1 Cor. 15:8–11). He who had persecuted the church was nonetheless given the chance to be a part of it. And then he says that the grace of God had not been given him in vain. He had worked harder than any of the other apostles—obviously Paul's old intensity and egotism were never completely overcome. But having said that, he immediately stopped himself and said, "But wait, that is not exactly the whole truth. In all this strenuous effort, it has not been just me at work, but Christ working in me." You have to have experienced this kind of creativity in order to understand it fully, but I am here to report that *there is something to it.* And the conviction has grown on me that the way the Beecher Lectures were done is a good way of doing all of life. The contract that was offered to me for that project is a contract I am prepared to sign for every day and every project. It is living the way Abraham was invited to live, the way all his creative sons and daughters have lived. This kind of life is available at this very moment to whoever is gripped by its promise and is willing to start learning the dance step of collaboration.

Now that I am several months beyond these events and can look back, it may be that the way these lectures came into being will have a more lasting impact on my life than what was said in them. At any rate, I have concluded that the story of the roots of these presentations was worth sharing, along with the fruits, and thus the reason for the lengthy introduction.

How does one ever formulate a proper and comprehensive "thanksgiving" for a project of this type? In a sense, I have been writing these lectures all my life, for what is contained here is a pulling together for the first time in print of experiences and insights that go back to my earliest days and were shaped by innumerable individuals. There is no way I could begin to identify specifically the ways in which "good-ness and mercy have followed me all the days of my life."

However, I must name a few individuals. Both Dean Colin Williams and Associate Dean Harry Adams were gracious and supportive throughout this whole process. Many of the faculty and students at both the divinity school and the university gave me warm encourage-ment by their attendance and their comments about the lectures. My dear colleague here in Jackson—Pat Travis—worked unstintingly in typing and retyping this material, and never once made me feel anything but her joy in having a part in this enterprise. That cheerful contribution was of tremendous benefit to me in "the six-week countdown" period. And last of all, I must affirm the role of my strong and wise wife Lue Ann in all of this. She at once encour-aged and challenged me—always letting me know that she felt I could and therefore I should be at my best for this project. Much of what I have become in the last twenty-six years is the result of interacting with this person of depth and excellence.

Thus, it is finished—this task of the Beecher Lectures for 1979. The event itself will remain for me a golden memory in my heart, and I hereby release this material into whatever future God chooses to give it. May it, and all of us, as Charles Williams would say, go under the Mercy[1]—forever.

JOHN R. CLAYPOOL

Jackson, Mississippi
June, 1979

1

The Preaching
Event

The Preaching Event

*I*t has been over two years now since the invitation to participate in the Beecher Lectures was graciously extended to me, and in this time I have put forth considerable effort to acquaint myself with this tradition. I must say that I have found it to be an enormously enriching experience. Not only have I learned a great deal about the art of preaching, but I have also encountered many delightful anecdotes along the way. One story came to me orally about a certain American divine who was invited to be the Beecher lecturer toward the end of his illustrious career—I believe he was in his sixties, if I remember correctly. He came to New Haven on Monday and had dinner with a small group of friends that night, one of whom was Halford Luccock. The lecturer went on and on about how he was having to pinch himself to realize this was actually happening—he felt so unworthy and almost in a dream to be in New Haven and at Yale for the Beecher Lectures. After considerable talk of this kind, there was a discreet pause, and then he said to Luccock: "But let me ask you one thing. Why did you wait so long?"

Let me acknowledge that my reactions on opening Dean Colin Williams's letter of invitation were exactly the opposite. I found myself saying, "Why didn't you wait a lot longer? There is so much about preaching I do not yet know . . . so many books that are yet to be read. If only I had twenty or thirty more years." But then, of course, it came to me: When would one ever feel ready for a responsibility of this magnitude? Is there ever a time when the desire to know more and possess clearer insight is not present?

From time to time I have tried to approach the Scriptures imaginatively and put myself in the place of certain individuals in the biblical account. On occasion I have focused on that lad and the crowd of five thousand with his loaves and fishes and wondered what he must have felt when he realized Jesus was asking for his lunch. I am confident his first reaction was one of surprise, quickly followed by a sense of regret. If only he had brought more or had a better lunch to offer! But that was beside the point at that moment. His choice was to keep what he had out of shame and selfishness or hand over trustingly what little he did possess. He followed the latter alternative, of course, and was amazed, with all the rest, at what that Mysterious Figure was able to do with so little. Very honestly, this is the frame of reference I am choosing to set around the Beecher Lectures of 1979. God knows I wish I had more and better wisdom to share, but such as I have, I now give to him and to you. What loaves and fishes of insight I have been given across the years, I now propose to make available, trusting that the One who was present then will be present now and will take my precious little and multiply as he will to the feeding of us all.

My study of the Beecher tradition suggests that two options lie open before each lecturer. Either one can talk about the task of preaching itself, or one can take some aspect of this gospel that we have been given and elaborate on that. After much consideration, I have chosen to walk down that first road, which means that I shall attempt to bring a highly provisional report of how I view the preaching task at this moment and what I deem to be some of its most important aspects. I have chosen to entitle these lectures *The Preaching Event*, for it is my deepest conviction that when one stands to engage in this particular act, far more takes place than the mere speaking and hearing of words. Preaching is at bottom what Phillips Brooks defined it to be in his memorable lectures of 1877. It is "the communication of truth through man to men," or as we would say it today, "through human personality to human personalities." Far more than the uttering and hearing of audible sounds is involved here. Authentic preaching catches up all the faculties of the human beings involved in the process—their minds and bodies and emotions as well as their tongues and ears. Thus it can rightly be called *an event*, something that happens so wholistically that it leaves the kind of impact on one that accompanies participation in any sort of decisive happening.

I remember having this concept of preaching brought home to me very vividly when I was a seminary student and went to an ecumenical conference at which D. T. Niles, the great Asian churchman, was to bring the principal address. He began in a surprising way. His first utterance was to ask those of us in the congregation to stand to our feet, turn and face the back of the sanctuary. We did this in a rather puzzled fashion. Then he told us to turn back around and face the front, which we did, and then to sit down again. By this time a murmur of confusion spread all over the room. Had this world-renowned preacher "fallen out of his tree" or lapsed into senility? Then Niles said: "I have begun in this fashion to demonstrate to you the power of the spoken word. As you have just witnessed, words make things happen. One person speaking to another involves far more than certain sounds being created and transmitted and heard. It is more like arrows or bullets being shot into a given place. Spoken words are units of energy. They go out to do things and make a difference in the realities they touch. Words are a form of deed," he asserted, and went on to suggest that what he had done in moving us around physically by the power of the spoken word was entirely in line with the Old Testament's understanding of the act of speaking. No culture ever held this particular form of human potency in higher regard than our Hebrew forefathers. They believed that once a word had been spoken, it became an entity in its own right, just like an arrow or a bullet, sent on its way to do whatever it would of good or evil.

This understanding helps clarify biblical incidents that otherwise are unintelligible to persons of a different culture. I remember as a child being read Bible stories by my mother and puzzling over the account where Jacob and his mother tricked blind old Isaac into giving him the blessing that rightfully belonged to Esau, the firstborn son. I could not understand why Isaac was so helpless when this conspiracy of deception was brought to light, but of course the answer lies in the Hebrew understanding of the spoken word! Once Isaac had said those words of blessing, they were loose in the world just like an arrow that had left the bow. It was beyond his power to recall them and to give that blessing to Esau. The poet is right:

Boys flying kites pull in their white-winged birds,
But this you cannot do, when you are flying words.
Thoughts unexpressed may someday fall back dead,
But God Himself can't kill them once they are said.[1]

The point is that something decisive really does occur when we speak a word into existence and then send it out into the world. William Temple once defined a human action as "the difference we make by what we do." In this sense, the action of the tongue in uttering a word is every bit as decisive a deed as an act of the hand or an act of the foot. Words are power, which is why I have dared to define the act of preaching as an "event." It is going to be my contention that when we do this authentically, something of enormous significance takes place. An event occurs, where power of the deepest sort moves out of one human being to affect other human beings.

Now to be sure, any form of human potency can be trivialized and misused and thus made to look futile and unimportant. And there is no denying that much has taken place in the name of preaching that has been of little significance. However, abuse is never the justification for abandonment, nor does it invalidate the whole process. I have witnessed preaching events, as I am sure you have, that were overwhelmingly powerful in their impact. Thus the questions that I shall be raising in the rest of these pages grow out of the belief that when this human endeavor is engaged in faithfully and in terms of its full potential, it represents one of the ways a human being can make a difference in the situation of other human beings as powerfully as any form of action open to humankind. Not only is it worth doing, it is worth doing well because of its enormous potential.

I propose, then, to come at the preaching

event from several fundamental angles. I am under no burden to try to be original here, for as C. S. Lewis reminds us, originality is not a prerogative of creaturehood—that gift belongs to God alone. My sharings come out of a quarter of a century of involvement in parish ministry, and will revolve around four of the most basic words of the English language: *what, why, how,* and *when.* The preaching event: *What* is it in terms of basic objective? *Why* is it done (the question of motivation)? *How* is it to be performed (the issue of methodology)? And lastly, *when* is it to be done (the question of timeliness)?

To the first of these questions, then, let us now turn.

2

The Preaching
Event:

What?

The Preacher as Reconciler

The first question I want to pose is the most fundamental of all—it has to do with the objective of the preaching event. No matter what you are doing, you have to begin with the foundational question: "What is my goal in this endeavor?" When Samuel Miller was being inaugurated as the dean of the Divinity School at Harvard, he used the words of Thomas Carlyle as his text: "If only we could find the point again." This reminds me of something Abraham Lincoln said as he assumed the presidency in a troubled time: "If we could first learn where we are and whither we are tending, we could then better judge what to do, and how to do it."[1]

35

These statements underline the significance of the question, "Exactly what is the preacher attempting to do when he or she stands up to deliver a sermon?"

I have been greatly helped at this point by the opening paragraphs of the Beecher Lectures of 1907 by the British Congregationalist, P. T. Forsyth.[2] He begins his famous series by distinguishing the work of the orator from that of the Christian preacher. The orator, he suggests, is intent on getting people to do certain things. The goal here is to motivate individuals and arouse them to act in a certain way. However, the goal of the Christian preacher is very different. His or her goal is to reestablish a relation of trust between the human creature and the ultimate Creator. Reconciliation of the profoundest sort is the true business of the preacher— somehow to facilitate a spirit of openness, trust, at-one-ment, at the deepest level where what is made and What has done the making come together.

According to the earliest accounts in the Book of Genesis, all the anguish we have known in history can be traced back to a single point. It reports that something awesome occurred at the beginning of our human saga. A spirit of mistrust came into being at the primal level, and once it had formed, all the disintegration and alienation that is the inevitable fruit of such a spirit began to work itself out.

I heard once about a merchant out in the Midwest who had identical twin sons. The boys' lives became inseparably intertwined. From the first they dressed alike, went to the same schools, did all the same things. In fact, they were so close that neither ever married, but they came back and took over the running of the family business when their father died. Their relationship to each other was pointed to as a model of creative collaboration.

One morning a customer came into the store and made a small purchase. The brother who waited on him put the dollar bill on top of the cash register and walked to the front door with the man. Some time later he remembered what he had done, but when he went to the cash register, he found the dollar gone. He asked his brother if he had seen the bill and put it into the register, and the brother replied that he knew nothing of the bill in question.

"That's funny," said the other, "I distinctly remember placing the bill here on the register, and no one else has been in the store since then."

Had the matter been dropped at that point—a

mystery involving a tiny amount of money—nothing would have come of it. However, an hour later, this time with a noticeable hint of suspicion in his voice, the brother asked again, "Are you sure you didn't see that dollar bill and put it into the register?" The other brother was quick to catch the note of accusation, and flared back in defensive anger.

This was the beginning of the first serious breach of trust that had ever come between these two. It grew wider and wider. Every time they tried to discuss the issue, new charges and countercharges got mixed into the brew, until finally things got so bad that they were forced to dissolve their partnership. They ran a partition down the middle of their father's store and turned what had once been a harmonious partnership into an angry competition. In fact, that business became a source of division in the whole community, each twin trying to enlist allies for himself against the other. This open warfare went on for over twenty years.

Then one day a car with an out-of-state license drove up in front of the store. A well-dressed man got out and went into one of the sides and inquired how long the merchant had been in business in that location. When he found that it was over twenty years, the stranger said, "Then you are the one with whom I must settle an old score.

"Some twenty years ago," he said, "I was out of work, drifting from place to place, and I happened to get off a box car in your town. I had absolutely no money and had not eaten for three days. As I was walking down the alley behind your store, I looked in and saw a dollar bill on the top of the cash register. Everyone else was in the front of the store. I had been raised in a Christian home and I had never before in all my life stolen anything, but that morning I was so hungry I gave in to the temptation, slipped through the door and took that dollar bill. That act has weighed on my conscience ever since, and I finally decided that I would never be at peace until I came back and faced up to that old sin and made amends. Would you let me now replace that money and pay you whatever is appropriate for damages?"

At that point the stranger was surprised to see the old man standing in front of him shaking his head in dismay and beginning to weep. When he had gotten control of himself, he took the stranger by the arm and said, "I want you to go next door and repeat the same story you have just told me." The stranger did it, only this time there were two old men who looked remarkably alike, both weeping uncontrollably.

To think—twenty years of hostility and recrimination and destruction! And it all rooted back to a spirit of mistrust that came to exist between them, a mistrust which tragically enough was now revealed as having no basis in reality at all!

This story illustrates dramatically what a spirit of mistrust and suspicion can do to relationships. Wherever it takes root, disintegration and alienation are sure to follow. And of course, what happened in our own century in a tiny midwestern town parallels the biblical account of what went wrong at the beginning of our human life in history.

There was a time, you see, when the Creator and the ones he had created lived together like those twin brothers, in a state of collaboration and trust. The poetic image in the Book of Genesis is that of "walking together in the cool of the day," sharing in openness and gratitude and trust. But then, something happened to shatter that primal trust. What was it? For years I named the culprit "arrogance and disobedience." The stories of Genesis tell of an insurrection on the part of the creatures against the

Creator and his design. They set in motion a riot of unmaking that proceeded to turn back into chaos what God had so carefully fashioned into cosmos. Yes, there was open rebellion of the creatures against the Creator. But recently I found myself asking, "Why was this? What prompted those who had been created to break out of trustful oneness with their Source?" And then it dawned on me that beneath the disobedience was the cancerous shadow of suspicion. The human creatures turned against their Creator for the same reason that that one twin turned against the other: because *a spirit of mistrust had taken root at the deepest level.*

In the Genesis account, it was the serpent who suggested it first. He was the one who entered the scene and ever so subtly began to cast aspersions on the motives of the Creator. "Did he tell you to eat of this and not to eat of that?" was his inquiry. When the creatures answered innocently, "Yes," and repeated back the Creator's instructions, he went on to say, "Don't you see what is happening? How can you be so stupid? This One who is giving you all these instructions—don't you realize who he is? He is an exploiter, an insecure tyrant who needs to hold you down in order to prop himself up. He knows, you see, that if you eat of that fruit he forbids, you will become exactly as he is. You will not need to listen to all his dos and don'ts anymore. You will be free to be a god in your own right. If you know what is good for you, you will see him as the enemy that he is. You will recognize that he is the obstacle to your true fulfillment. Have done, then, with such oppression! Go to war! Take things into your own hands. Whatever he forbids, grasp. Whenever he says, 'Turn left,' turn right. You are under siege, creatures, in the grip of a devouring enemy. To keep on trusting is to be devoured. To rebel is your only hope."

Thus came the awesome moment when the oneness of innocence dissolved into the anxiety of choice, and the tragedy of all tragedies is that in that moment our human forbears did exactly what that twin brother chose to do—they sided with suspicion rather than trust. They chose to believe the worst rather than the best, and that is how The Great Unmaking that our forefathers called "The Fall" was set in motion. Once it was decided that the Source could not be trusted, then everything began to unravel. Conflict and estrangement became the order of the day. The distrustful creatures began to take life apart and started trying to put it together again in ways that had nothing to do with the original design.

It is not surprising that all kinds of chaos resulted. In the beginning God had started with nothing, and then through chaos had slowly worked to bring order and beauty and cosmos into being. But the spirit of dissatisfaction that had been loosed by primal mistrust proceeded to reverse this process, and the great unmaking that turns cosmos back into chaos began and finally came to encompass the whole of reality.

Transactional Analysis has devised a spectrum that begins at zero and proceeds positively and negatively in opposite directions. On the one hand is minus one, minus two, minus three, minus four, minus five. On the other side is plus one, plus two, plus three, plus four, plus five. The negative spectrum moves from "I'm not O.K." to "You're not O.K." to "We're not O.K." to "They're not O.K." to "It's not O.K." This is a modern restatement of how the spirit of mistrust finally moves to contaminate every particle of reality. Once it is decided that the Source of all things is The Enemy—that which is against us and cannot be trusted—then everything he has done falls under this shadow of suspicion. When that spirit of panic was set in motion, the paradisiacal harmony that once existed in the Garden dissolved into a riot of estrangement.

These are the primordial images that the Bible

sets as the background of our human situation then and now. They raise the question, "Can anything be done about this riot of unmaking that is raging at this moment within and all about each one of us?" Is it possible—to use again the story of the twins in the Midwest—that someone could come, like the stranger with the out-of-state license, and set right what had gone wrong by shedding new light on an old situation? Back then a man came with a certain story to tell whose impact was incredible. By what he told it suddenly became clear that the mistrust which had set in motion so much division and emotional destruction was, in fact, mistaken. The suspicion that had led to accusation and counteraccusation had in truth been misplaced all along. Is it possible that someone could come and do for our human situation of estrangement what that stranger did for those twins and ultimately for that whole community?

It is my contention that this is not only possible, but that right here is the ultimate objective of the preaching event. Remember what P. T. Forsyth said: it is the task of the orator to motivate people to act in a certain way, while the task of the preacher is something far more profound. The preacher is to work to reestablish a relation of trust at the deepest level between human creatures and the Ultimate Creator. And what better image can you use than the image of that stranger, entering an arena of strife with a story that goes all the way down to the basics and all the way back to the beginning, and has the power to set right what initially had gone wrong? This is the work of a reconciler, one of the primal images of the Christian ministry. This is who we are to be and what we are to do!

But what is the story we have to tell? It begins in the very beginning with the image of a God who found his own aliveness so overwhelmingly joyful that he decided it was too good to keep to himself. "I want others to taste something of this ecstasy I am experiencing," he said. "Therefore, I will create, not in order to get something for myself, but in order to give something of myself. I will call into being creatures who are capable of my kind of joy."

Thus the story begins with an image of primal joy and the assertion that creation was at bottom an act of generosity, not an act of selfishness. The fear that we humans ultimately have to do with an exploitive Reality simply is not true. But one does not have to take that assertion merely on faith. Look at what this God of joy did, not only in creation, but after the riot of suspicion broke out and the creatures he had intended to bless turned against him in rebellion. The towering miracle is that he did not allow himself to be drawn into that angry war dance—as did the accused twin—and return hostility for hostility. Rather, he set about immediately to allay the suspicions of his creatures by acting decisively and lovingly in history.

John Killinger once commented that "Jesus was God's answer to the problem of a bad reputation." In a sense that is true, if you see Jesus as the climax of a long process, not merely as an isolated event. The truth is, God began to answer this problem of a bad reputation in his dealings with Abraham and subsequently with Israel. This man Abraham, who had been schooled in the structures of suspicion—how amazed he must have been to find himself encountered by a God called Yahweh and to learn that here was a Deity who wanted to bless, to give, to fulfill, not to manipulate or exploit! In the God who said, "I want to give you a land to call your own, descendants more numerous than the sands of the sea, a name that will be made great throughout history, and a means by which all the families of the earth shall bless themselves," the reality of gift-love enters history once again—the same kind of gift-love that stands in the beginning and desires to create, not for what he can get for himself but for what he can give of himself. You see it all over again, in the life of a man and then in the life of a nation—God answering the charges that had been leveled at him by the serpent, and working to show that at heart he is for and not against his creation, Someone to be trusted, not to be feared. But Killinger is right—this Reality took its most dramatic and incredible form in the person of Jesus of Nazareth. In an attempt to get at the problem of a bad reputation, God spared not his own Son, but offered him up for us all.

I must confess to you that I had never fully understood the depth of this image until I became a parent myself and began to feel all of those protective urges we have for our own flesh and blood. Since then I have tended to regard the welfare of my only son as a value above almost any other value. Thus, the thought of deliberately letting him suffer or of sacrificing him in behalf of someone or something else— such a prospect is absolutely mind-boggling. And yet the story we Christian preachers have to tell is significant for this very reason.

I can still remember the time when this aspect of the Easter story hit me with full intensity. For the purposes of illustration, I began to imagine that a certain tenant family was having all kinds of problems, and I had resolved to do what I could to help them. I arranged to have them move onto some land I owned, and into a house that I provided. I went out and tried to teach them the skills that went with making a living on a farm, and I provided the money for the seed and the equipment for farming. I set them up so at last they could have a chance to live creatively. But very soon it became apparent that these persons were not responding positively to what I had done. They were not working. They were wrecking the house that I had provided them. They were tearing up the machinery and using the money intended for seed to buy liquor. However, I did not give up. I continued to reason with them. I sent out the county agent and other people who might be able to help, and patiently stayed with my goal of helping these people out of the condition they had gotten themselves into. But things only got worse.

Finally, in my imagination, my only son said to me, "Perhaps there is a way I can get to them. They know who I am. I have a special feel for some of the younger members of the family. Perhaps if I went out and spent some time with them, we could reverse the trend and get them on the right track."

And so, with no small misgiving, I agreed to let him go. And two days later the word comes back, "They took your son in and received him cordially at first. But then very quickly their mood changed, and they became sullen and hostile. Just yesterday they took him out behind the barn, tied his hands and tortured him for a while, and then killed him in cold blood."

As I allowed myself to feel the emotions of such a situation, I found a primitive rage building up in me against the creatures who would do this sort of thing. My first impulse was to unleash all the hurtful and destructive powers within me against such utter ingrates. I had to admit that if it had been in my power to raise my son back from the dead, it would never in a thousand years have occurred to me to send him back to the kind of creatures who had treated him this way.

At that point, the miracle of the Easter event broke over me. It was not just the power of God that astonished me here—the ability to take something that had been killed and call it back to life again. That is amazing. But even more amazing is the patience and mercy of a God who would still have hope for the kind of creatures who had treated his only begotten Son that way. Three days after human beings killed him in cold blood, the word was out, not only that he was alive again, but that he was saying, "I go before you into Galilee. Let's keep on keeping on. Let's get back to the task of dispelling suspicion and reconciling the world back to the Father as he really is." That is the towering miracle of Easter that broke in on me that day.

The story the Christian preacher has to tell is the story of a God whose only reason for creating was his desire to share the wonder of his aliveness and who, in the face of utterly erroneous suspicion, has refused to stop loving or to give up on creation, but moves to repair the damage and to affirm again that he really is for us and not against us. If trust at the deepest level could ever be reestablished, if that which has gone wrong can ever be set right, does not this story have the potential to do it? Working to bring this story to bear on the place of the primal break is the true objective of the preacher. To be sure, we are called on to do many things and to avail ourselves of a variety of strategies, but at bottom we are ministers of reconciliation. The task of the orator is to get human beings to do certain things, to rouse them to a particular action, but the task of the preacher is something far different. His or her objective is to reestablish a relation of trust at the deepest level between the human creature and the Creator. If healing could come here, if somehow the light of God's true nature could penetrate all the way back and all the way down to the place of our suspicion, can you not see what tremendous effect this could have, what action it could inspire?

Earlier I outlined the Transactional Analysis spectrum that moved step by step in a negative direction. As I mentioned, it has a positive counterpoint: "I'm O.K. You're O.K. We're O.K. They're O.K. It's O.K." If we could only come to trust again, we could begin to move in this positive direction. If it finally got through to us that our Ultimate Source is positive and not negative, One who can be trusted and collaborated with, not One who needs to be fought and opposed, then we would be roused to act differently. We would be able to feel differently, because the connection at the basis of our being would be made whole again, and the delight that God wanted us to know from the beginning could start to flow again.

The Christian preacher, then, does have an awesome task to perform. He or she must attempt to do far more than simply move people around at the level of behavior. Our task is to reestablish trust at the deepest level, to participate in the miracle of primal reconciliation. I am convinced it is the thing the world most needs. We have been given a story which has the power to do for all human beings what that out-of-state stranger did for two estranged brothers. It can shed new light on an old wound, show us how wrong we have been in our suspicion of our Maker, and reestablish trust at the deepest level. Could any work in all the world be more important?

I think not. Here am I, Lord. Send me!

3

The Preaching
Event:

Why?

The Preacher as Gift-Giver

Of all the questions that come to mind in relation to the preaching event, by far the most disturbing to me is the single word *why?* I am thinking now about the issue of motivation. What on earth is harder, really, than being totally honest at this point? When I stand up to preach, or to participate in any form of ministry, for that matter, why am I engaging in such an effort? Am I attempting to get something for myself or am I attempting to give something of myself?

C. S. Lewis described the first alternative by the term "need-love."[1] This is a process that is born of emptiness and thus reaches out hungrily

55

to any object that seems to hold the promise of filling it. Need-love is like a vacuum. It is forever sucking into itself those things that it desires or wants. If an attempt were made to chart this process, it would turn out to look like a circle— that is, loving going out from subject to object for the purpose of bringing something back from object to subject. The goal here is always the transfer of value from object back to the subject, which means that need-love is essentially acquisitive and intent on building itself up at the expense of all that it touches.

When such a process is so described, who among us can claim to be a stranger to it or begin to number the times and places when this was exactly the name of the game we were playing with people and ideas and institutions and even God himself? Need-love is perhaps the most pervasive single activity in which human beings engage. But it is by no means our only capability.

There is also such a thing as "gift-love," Lewis says, which is radically different from what I have just described. Here the goal is to enhance the value of the object, not to diminish it. Gift-love is born of fullness rather than emptiness, and desires to share of itself rather than to take for itself. It is more like an artesian well than a

Negative flux [handwritten marginalia]

vacuum. Its purpose is to transfer value, not from object back to subject, but rather from subject to object. An attempt to chart this process would look more like an arc than a circle. The ultimate desire here is to build up rather than tear down. Instead of being acquisitive and exploitive, this process is at bottom generous and creative.

Now the moments when this description fits what human beings are doing may be much rarer indeed than the former process, but the truth is, we humans have it in us to show gift-love as well as need-love. That fact raises the awesome question: "When I stand up to preach a sermon, which one of these terms rightly describes what I am doing? Am I trying to get something from the audience for myself, or am I intent on giving something of myself to the audience?" Who has the courage even to raise such an issue in his or her heart of hearts, much less to dig deep for an answer?

I once heard Father John Powell recount an experience that brought this issue home to me existentially. It seems the Archbishop of Chicago asked Powell and two other theologians to visit the various schools in the diocese and conduct a symposium on the subject of spiritual formation. Their tour ended back at Loyola University, on whose faculty Powell himself serves. Here were the people with whom he worked everyday and who knew him best. Father Powell said as he sat on the platform watching the audience gather, a great sense of heaviness swept over him, an almost suffocating feeling of immobility. Powell is a very intuitive person, so instead of swallowing or evading these feelings, he dared to live into them right there on the stage, and attempted to trace them back to their source. When he did this, the impression came to him: "You are getting ready to put on a dazzling performance. Your goal is to try to impress these people, get them to see how brilliant and well-versed you are in your chosen discipline. Your intention is to get something from them, to win their praise, when in fact what they really need is not a dazzling performance at all, but a gift of love, whatever warmth and insight that has been given to you that might be a resource to them for their journey."

It was a sobering moment indeed, Father Powell said, to have a mirror held up to his ultimate motivation on that occasion. I must report that I began to shift uncomfortably in my seat as he told this, because it brought back a string of memories out of my own past and reminded me again of what has been the central struggle of my entire existence.

For reasons that I am at a loss to account for fully, my beginning point in self-awareness was decidedly negative in tone. Karen Horney has suggested that "basic anxiety about one's self" is the root problem with most neurotics.[2] If this is true, I would certainly qualify for that label. For you see, from the very beginning, I did not like the way I came from the hand of the Creator. I imaged myself as an emptiness, a big fat zero, one who somehow did not measure up as I was. I can really identify with the main character in Charles Schulz's comic strip "Peanuts." Again and again in the figure of Charlie Brown I see a depiction of my own childhood. I particularly remember one episode in which Charlie was lamenting to his friend Linus about his chronic, lifelong sense of insecurity. "It goes all the way back to the beginning," he said. "The moment I was born and stepped on the stage of history, they took one look at me and said, 'Not right for the part.'" Not even Karen Horney could have given a better definition of basic anxiety.

As I said, I am at a loss to trace out all the causes of this self-despising. I do remember that again and again in my early days I was told: "If you are ever going to amount to anything, you have to make something of yourself." Here is a good case of intention and consequence getting out of synchronization. I am sure those who said this meant it to be a source of motivation—that is, to inspire me to make the most of what I had been given. However, as educator Rudolf Dreikurs has pointed out, "Children are often excellent observers but poor interpreters." They hardly miss a thing when it comes to taking it all in, but drawing the correct conclusions is another thing. In my case, I took these words as an assessment of my condition rather than as a challenge to my potential. I interpreted them to mean: "As you are just now, John Claypool, you do *not* amount to anything, and if there is ever going to be any significance to your life, you are going to have to go somewhere else and import it and become something other than what you are right now." I am not attempting to place the blame for this bad beginning on someone else. Each one of us is responsible, I believe, for the images of self that we fashion out of the raw material of our earliest experiences. I was the one who decided that as I came up "from the gates of the morning,"[3] I was not good enough as I was. And as I reflect upon it, two devastating effects proceeded to grow from this way I chose to image myself initially.

For one thing, it affected me profoundly at the feeling level. A mood of dissatisfaction settled over my whole existence and became the vantage point from which I interpreted everything. Someone pointed out to me not long ago that Jesus' famous words, "Thou shalt love thy neighbor as thyself," are as much a statement of a psychological fact as they are an ethical imperative. The truth is: *we will love our neighbors as we love ourselves!* The pattern we develop of relating to that person closest to us, namely ourselves, becomes the paradigm of the way we will relate to all other people. You see, if I really do not like myself and am critical and hostile and dissatisfied with the very first part of creation that I experience, then it follows that I am going to perceive all others through these same lenses and will proceed to relate to them as I relate to myself. If we could look to the bottom of the raging dissatisfaction that characterizes so many people today, chances are it all goes back to a dislike of self that has a way of poisoning everything else one perceives.

Winston Churchill used to tell the story of the British family that went out for a picnic by a lake. In the course of the afternoon the five-year-old son fell into the water. Unfortunately, none of the adults could swim. As the child was bobbing up and down and everyone on the shore was dissolving in panic, a passerby saw the situation. At great risk to himself he dived in fully clothed and managed to reach the child just before he went under for the third time. He was able to pull him out of the water and present him safe and sound to his mother. Instead of thanking this stranger for his heroic efforts, however, the mother snapped peevishly at the rescuer, "Where's Johnny's cap?"[4] Somehow in all of this commotion, the boy's hat had gotten lost. Out of all the facets of that episode, the woman found something with which to be dissatisfied! If that is not the essence of neurosis, I do not know what is.

Yet the truth is that dissatisfaction, like charity, usually begins at home. When the first conclusion you draw about yourself is decidedly negative, that has a way of poisoning all the rest. As I pointed out earlier, when the position "I'm not O.K." is staunchly assumed, it will not be long until "You're not O.K.," "We're not O.K.," "They're not O.K.," and "It's not O.K." will follow. My own recollection of childhood richly confirms this. The feeling that I did not amount to anything as I was, served to contaminate the whole atmosphere of my existence at a feeling level.

The other effect was what this negative self-image prompted me to do at the behavioral level. Once I came to the conclusion that as I was

I did not amount to anything, the question arose: "What can I do about this? How does a nobody become a somebody? How does my kind of emptiness get filled with the density of significance?" Had I been born in another culture, perhaps the answer to that question would have been different. But since my context of "coming to be" was America and I was white, middle-class, and male to boot, the answer to that inquiry was not hard to find. It was summed up in one word: "Compete!" The command was "Achieve! Go out there and pit yourself against other people and do what you must to come out ahead! The name of the game is 'King of the Mountain.' The thing to do is to climb over everybody's back until at last you get up to the top."

Arthur Miller has captured this cultural ideal graphically in the tragic figure of Willy Loman,[5] who was driven all his life by one dream and one dream only—"to come out number one man," to emerge out of the heap chanting ecstatically, "I'm number one, I'm number one, I'm number one!" Although I certainly did not process all this intellectually, at an exceedingly early age I became what might be classified technically as "Homo competetus." The overwhelming drive of my life became "to make it," "to get ahead," "to out-achieve all others" so as to do something about that awful emptiness I sensed at the bottom of my being.

This way of living affected me at every level. It invaded even my fantasy world. People used to ask me what I wanted to be when I grew up, and I was shrewd enough to fashion my answer according to what I thought they wanted to hear. For some it was a policeman, for others a fireman or a preacher. However, in my own heart of hearts, I had my own private fantasy that I never dared to share with anyone. Do you know what it was? I am telling you the gospel truth: *I wanted to be president of the world!* I envisioned the whole human race as a giant pyramid with one place of preeminence at the top. I dreamed of climbing over everybody's back until at last I got there. Then I knew exactly what I would do. I would look down and say, "Now! Now, do I amount to something? Have I at last become a somebody out of my nobodiness?"

But all of that, mind you, was reserved for the realm of fantasy. In the concrete world of everyday life, I was utterly pragmatic and manipulative. In the early grades, I learned how to maneuver my way into becoming the teacher's pet—the one who got to wash the blackboards during recess and take notes to the principal's office while others sat in reading circles. Later on those heroic figures called Safety Patrolmen caught my eye. These were sixth-grade boys who wore white belts across their chests and got to stand in high visibility at street corners and say to others, "Go," and they would go, or "Stop," and they would stop. Getting to that level of power became my next challenge, and I was successful—only to discover what was to become a recurring pattern; namely, that as soon as you achieve one goal, you find another looming up before you. There turned out to be an elite within the elite, a captain and a lieutenant among the ordinary heroes. And unfortunately Billy Depere's mother had a better "in" with the principal than my mother, so the best I could do was to make lieutenant—a word to this day I cannot spell, because I did not need to learn it. All I had to do was look down on my chest and there it was imprinted on that badge!

As life moved on, the number and forms of challenge escalated and became more complex. In junior high school there were athletic teams to be made, homeroom offices for which to run, grade point averages to think about and keep up, and by the time I had finished high school, I had become a seasoned veteran in the competitive wars of the human race. By untiring effort and manipulation, I had managed to be fairly successful. I remember not only taking pride in what I was accomplishing but beginning to experience the shadow side of this approach to life—that is, the contempt one comes to feel for those who have not fared as well.

I still remember the day a certain classmate of mine asked me if I would like to double date the next weekend. I needed a ride, so I quickly accepted his offer. But as I watched him walk down the hall, I remember saying to myself, "So-and-so, you really do have your gall, asking a girl for a date. You have never made any athletic team. You only make Cs. You have never been elected even treasurer of your home-room. So-and-so, you are a nothing." I realize now that I had come to the place of equating doing with being—that there was nothing to a person except what he or she was able to achieve.

I must pause at this point and note that none of the religious experiences of my early life began to touch the depths about which I am speaking now. At the age of nine, I was baptized into a Baptist church and remember feeling the warmth of those waters of immersion that were interpreted to me as God's love. But that warmth did not penetrate anywhere close to the emptiness I felt at the center of my being. In my adolescence, I had a prolonged period of intellectual doubt about which I will speak more fully later on. Yet even in the resolution that came to this dilemma—significant as it was to me—I continued to image myself as a nobody who had to compete and out-achieve all others in order to become a somebody.

This self-image persisted through college, into my decision to become a minister, and through my experience of seminary training. I have no way of knowing what other theological institutions are like, but my perception of the one I attended was that of a community of grades rather than a community of grace. The way we students interacted with each other and the professors reminds me of an incident in Jesus' life (Mark 9:33–37). He and his disciples were walking along together, and when they arrived at Capernaum, Jesus asked, "What were you all talking about back there on the road?" Everyone got red in the face and fell silent. When he finally dug it out of them, it turned out that they had been arguing about which of them would be the greatest, who would get to sit on Jesus' right hand and on his left hand when the time of glory arrived. You see, the rat race that we talk so much about in the twentieth century is by no means a new phenomenon. It has been going on since human beings first imaged themselves as insufficient and began to compete. And it is in this way that I remember my seminary days. Those of us who were most aggressive realized that sitting next to us were the persons with whom we would be competing for jobs for the rest of our careers. While the issue was never openly faced, the kind of jockeying that took place on the road to Capernaum is what took place in my seven years of seminary preparation.

I must say, also, that life in the parish ministry has not been a whole lot different. I can still recall going to state and national conventions in our denomination and coming home feeling drained and unclean, because most of the conversation in the hotel rooms and the halls was characterized either by envy of those who were doing well or scarcely concealed delight for those who were doing poorly. For did that not mean that someone was about to fall, and would thus create an opening higher up the ladder?

This is the way I basically approached life from the earliest moments of self-awareness until I reached my middle thirties. At that time, although I had never heard of Daniel Levinson and the concept of "the seasons of a man's life," or Gail Sheehy's image of "passages,"[6] I suppose what I encountered was the mid-adult crisis. At any rate, the obsession that had driven me since my earliest days gradually began to wane a bit. What happens here, Levinson says, is that the imbalances of our earlier days begin to make themselves felt. The parts of our lives in which we have overinvested no longer prove as satisfying as they once did, while those parts of ourselves that we have not nourished properly begin to cry out for attention.

About ten years out of the seminary I began to feel a variety of disquieting emotions. For one thing, I was really bone-weary. Do you have any idea how much energy it takes always to have to succeed and come out number one? I was also beginning to sense how lonely and isolated this way of living leaves one. How can you really relate openly and warmly to persons when you realize that at a deeper level you are competing with them and trying to outdo them? As I began to reflect more deeply on where I had been and where I was going, I remember saying to myself, "There has got to be a better way to live than this. There has got to be a more authentic form of well-being than this relentless need to compete and out-achieve." But where was it?

And then two events happened in rapid succession that were to have a lasting impact on my life.

The first of these was an event of judgment. It occurred in a most unlikely setting, the meeting of a Kiwanis Club in a downtown hotel in Louisville, Kentucky. I had gone that day very ritualistically, because you have to attend a certain number of times or else you are put out. I never expected in a thousand years for something of ultimate significance to occur to me that day. The speaker was the personnel manager of a national firm.

In the course of his remarks, he told us that the first thing he tried to determine about a new employee was whether that individual was intent on "being something" or on "doing something." Elaborating on this distinction, he said, "The individual who is intent on being something is a person who does not have his or her ego needs met healthily. Such employees are forever attempting to use the job in order to enhance themselves. These are people who are never able to risk anything or act courageously. All of their moves tend to be manipulative. When they come up to a given problem, they always perceive it on two levels. On the surface, they are asking, 'What needs to be done here?'

But at a deeper level, they are asking, 'How can I use this situation to get ahead myself?' These people have flawed vision, and very frankly, the higher they get in the decision-making process, the more and more of a liability they become.

"On the other hand, the individual who wants to do something is a person who has his or her ego needs met healthily. In a sense, individuals like these have themselves off their hands, so they are able to come to a problem situation and ask the single question, 'What needs to be done here?' These individuals are able to sacrifice. They are able to take risks. They are able to make the hard decisions. And although they are rare indeed, the quicker I can identify them and move them up the decision-making hierarchy, the better it is for the business in years to come."

I had never heard this particular distinction made before. But as that man spoke about these two kinds of individuals, I felt just like King David must have felt when Nathan held up a mirror to his inner being and said: "Thou art the man." In the image of the person who needs to be something, I saw a reflection of my own true self. In fact, I could not suppress the feeling: "All your life, this has been who you are and how you have done things."

In that moment, all kinds of memories began

to flood my mind. I thought of the times I had gone to speak at a denominational meeting and had sat down after my talk thinking, on one level, "I hope I did what the people who invited me wanted." But at a deeper level I would be asking, "I wonder if they were impressed. Perhaps there is someone here with influence who will remember the name of this young comer, and tonight will be a stepping stone up the ladder of success."

I remembered the times that I had not really been able to reach out and identify with another's need because my own need to be approved was so overwhelming. I served for eleven years in a church adjacent to a seminary campus. Every fall a crop of new students would come and there would be a rash of counseling appointments. One September a first-year student came in to talk about some of his dilemmas. The first thing he said was, "I do not know why I have come to talk to you, really, because to be honest I cannot stand to hear you preach. You have this funny inflection in your voice that just drives me up the wall." Then he went on to talk about the problems he was facing. To be honest with you, I did not hear a word he said for five minutes, because I was so busy putting Band-Aids on my wounded ego. This man did not think I was a great preacher! Thus I was totally incapable of getting in touch with his pain because of my own wounded self-image.

Experience after experience like these came to my mind, and I walked out of the Kiwanis Club meeting that day staggered by an insight into myself that I had never recognized before.

But what do you do when you discover such a massive flaw as this? Where do you go for help? This was my quandary. Then—and not by coincidence, I am convinced, but by Providence—a second event occurred that was to have a positive impact. It began with a telephone call from a Presbyterian minister in Louisville. He was in real personal anguish, he said, and he asked the question: "Where does a pastor go for pastoral care? We are so busy helping other people. Where do we turn when our needs become overwhelming?

"At any rate," he continued, "I am calling five of you whom I trust with this request. Would you agree to meet with me in my study once a week for six times? The only contract will be that we will try to be honest and hear each other. Perhaps we can develop enough trust so that we can take off our masks and show each other where we really hurt. And maybe we can become a band of brothers who can bequeath healing and encouragement to each other. I do not know if this will work, but if it does not, I'll go under for sure!"

I was frankly startled when that conversation was over, because I had only known this man from a distance, and he appeared to be "so together" that I would never have dreamed in a thousand years that he was struggling as he indicated. Then, too, I had a sense of foreboding about the group he proposed. I was not at all sure that I could stay in the role of the helper in that kind of context. I had the fear that I might step over the line and take off my mask and let some of these wounds that I had just discovered become visible. And to be honest, the group he mentioned were ministers with whom I felt a great deal of competition. I wanted them to see me as a winner, not as the person I was slowly discovering myself to be. Therefore, it was not at all easy for me to decide what to do. But I suppose if one is hurting badly enough, he or she will do almost anything.

So the next morning I went to that man's study and touched for the first time in my life an experience of genuine *koinonia*. I was absolutely astonished by what began to unfold before my eyes. For one thing, I discovered that every one of us around that table was struggling with much the same problems. Miguel Unamuno, the Spanish philosopher, once said that if we ever got honest enough to go out in the streets and uncover our common grief, we would discover that we are all grieving for the selfsame things.[7] I had no idea that behind the façade of successful clergymen were some of the very same struggles that I was experiencing. We were all so much more alike than I had realized. Then, too, I was amazed to see that in that context honesty evoked compassion. Whenever a person was authentic enough to take off his mask and let his true condition be seen, instead of being condemned or exploited, I found all kinds of insight and concern flowed to him as response. I am aware that not all small groups function this way, but that particular group was remarkably healthy and therapeutic.

And so one morning, with all the courage that I could muster, I did something that I had never done before. I took off my mask. I related the story that I have shared today—about that old and deep sense of nobodiness, about how hard I had tried to make a name for myself and how weary and lonely and frustrated I had become. I did not realize myself how much pain there was inside until I began to share it and it gushed forth like the pus in a boil that at last has been lanced. When I had pretty much emptied myself, the man in the group for whom I felt the least natural affinity—an Episcopal rector who was well-born and had all the graces of Bluegrass aristocracy—was the first to speak.

"I hear you, John," he said, "I hear you. And I know exactly what you are talking about, because I am walking that road myself." Then he said, "Do you know what we need—not what *you* need, but what *we* need? We need to hear the gospel down in our guts. In the Sermon on the Mount, Jesus says, 'Ye are the light of the world.' He does not say, 'You have got to be number one in order to get light,' or, 'You must out-achieve everybody else in order to earn light.' He says simply, 'You are light.' If you and I," he went on, "could ever really experience that and believe it, then we could do what Jesus said. We could let our light shine, and people could see the good thing that God has created, and give glory to the Father in heaven."

I cannot explain why I had never heard that word of the gospel with my guts, for Lord knows I had read it many times, even in the original Greek. All I can report is that, in that moment, something like fire moved from the top of my head to the bottom of my heart! For the first time in my life, *I felt a sense of grace.* All of a sudden it dawned on me that I had been mistaken from that earliest moment of self-definition. The truth was—I did have worth in me from the beginning. And it was worth that resulted not from what I had to make of myself, but rather from what God had made of me when he called me out of nothing into being. The thought that I had to make something of myself if I was ever going to amount to anything had been the primal mistake. There had been worth in me from the moment I was created. It also dawned on me that the secret of life is not getting something outside inside by achieving and competing. It is, rather, getting what is already inside outside by acceptance and self-giving.

That morning, something akin to what happened to Martin Luther in his Tower experience and to John Wesley at Aldersgate happened to me in the study of a Presbyterian minister. My consciousness was altered irrevocably that day. I began to sense the grace that is the foundation of all things. That reality became more than a word or concept to me then—it took the form of an existential event.

My friend Sam Keen had a similar experience. He had always felt that if he could just get a doctorate from an Ivy League school and become a professor, then that sense of nobodiness that had been with him from the beginning would go away. But he accomplished all these goals only to find the same haunting emptiness within. One night alone in a hotel room, sophisticated modern man that he was, he found himself asking that old, old question, "What must I do to be saved?" And then, he said, the answer began to jump up and down before his eyes as if it were written on the wall. It was simply, "Nothing, nothing at all. It comes with the territory or it does not come at all." After that experience, he says, in looking back over his life, he realized he had been like a man "riding on an ox, looking for an ox."

What an apt image this is of life apart from a sense of grace! It describes me too: Here I was, looking everywhere in the realm of achievement for a way to amount to something, and all along the worth had been right there within me, but I had never realized it.

This was the beginning of a new way of perceiving reality for me, beginning with myself and moving out until all of reality was bathed by this gracious light. The old sense of dissatisfaction that went back to the first thing God ever did for me gave way to delight. I began to taste what the Genesis account suggests was God's feeling for what he had created—namely, delight, that childlike wonder that looks at what it has made and says ecstatically, "It is good, good, very, very good." I began to learn that things do not have to be perfect to be good, and compared with never having been at all, whatever one has been dealt in the act of creation is worthy of celebration.

I also experienced transformation at the level of doing as well. Slowly but surely it began to dawn on me that every gift I had been given would make a good present for someone else, and that sharing out of the fullness that was already in me by the grace of creation was far more redemptive than needing to get something from people through competition.

It was at this point, I would say, that ministry as a form of gift-love rather than need-love began to be a possibility for me. And I cannot begin to describe what a difference that made, not only inside me and what I felt in the process, but also in the impact that it had upon others. Let's face it: the preacher knows in his or her heart of hearts, and I think the congregation senses also, when a sermon is aimed primarily at getting or giving. Now to be sure, the words may be the same and the outward appearance is almost identical, but it is one kind of transaction to be taken from, and another thing to be given to. My point is that the preaching event will never be what it was meant to be until we who do it get in touch with primal grace, and thus are released from needing to be something in order to establish our sense of worth and are free to do something—that is, to let our light shine, so others can see the good thing God has done, and give glory to the Source of it all.

This is when the preaching event becomes what it was meant to be—when we who have come to see our very selves as gifts can turn to be gift-givers to others. If what I do in the pulpit is in fact making available to you that which has enriched me, then the whole process becomes free and creative. It means I can survive even if you do not like or accept my gift, for the agenda here is not for you to enhance me by your praise, but for me to enhance you as I can. This is when preaching has its moments of ecstasy and participates in primal creativity. This is when we actualize what it means to be made in the image of God.

The central affirmation of the Bible is that God's love is gift-love and not need-love. God did not have to create. There was no necessity outside himself, no gun to his head that forced him so to act. No, he created because he wanted to. Creation represents the overflowing of full-ness, not the hunger of emptiness. God's agenda is always to enhance value, not to extract it. Thus, when that sense of grace becomes the foundation of all things—our very lives, what we feel and what we do—then preaching as a form of gift-love becomes possible. I go into the pulpit to give something of myself, not to get something for myself. In so doing, I participate anew in the drama of grace that is the basis of all things, now and forevermore. By the grace of God, I am what I am and do what I do! And when this is the answer to the question, "The Preaching Event—Why?" one can expect re-markable creativity to follow.

4

The Preaching
Event:

How?

The Preacher as Witness

*I*n the last few years, no single book on the practice of ministry has been of more help to me than one written by a member of the faculty here at the Yale Divinity School. I am referring to Father Henri Nouwen's volume, *The Wounded Healer.*[1] I was particularly helped by the old legend out of the Talmud from which the image of the title is drawn.

Rabbi Yoshua Ben Levi came upon Elijah, the prophet, and asked him, "When will the Messiah come?"

Elijah replied, "Go, and ask him yourself."

"Where is he?" the rabbi asked.

"Sitting at the gates of the city."

"But, how shall I know him?"

"He is sitting among the poor, covered with wounds. The others unbind all their wounds at the same time and then bind them up again, but he unbinds only one at a time and binds it up again, saying to himself, 'Perhaps I shall be needed; if so, I must always be ready, so as not to delay for a moment.'"

What came together for me in this image was the realization that the secret of ministry consists of two things: first, the faithful tending of one's own woundedness, and second, the willingness to move to the aid of another and make the fruits of one's own woundedness available to others.

This principle seems to me to be applicable to all phases of ministry, but particularly to the preaching event and to the aspect of it that I want now to address—namely, how do we do this awesome task? What methodology is appropriate for such an endeavor? Up to this point, I have asked the questions *what* and *why* of the preaching event. Now I want to focus on the little word *how*, recognizing full well that it will be impossible in one chapter to speak exhaustively on such a subject. I would like to advance a single suggestion concerning methodology. It is this: *We will make our greatest impact in preaching when we dare to make available to the*

woundedness of others what we have learned through
an honest grappling with our own woundedness.

Instead of trying to dazzle people with the
breadth of our learning or to pass on lots of
secondhand information that may or may not be
existentially relevant to their situations, I can
help most when I am honest enough to lay bare
my own wounds and acknowledge what is
saving and helping me. Truth that I have found,
or better still, truth that has found me—this is
the sort of material that rightly belongs in the
preaching event. Lloyd Ogilvie once observed
that only the things that have happened to us
can happen through us.[2] I believe this is correct.
One of the qualities that gives authenticity and
urgency to our preaching is our own involvement in the very realities we proclaim. D. T.
Niles's image of the preacher as one starving
beggar telling other starving beggars where he
or she has found bread is a good one. There is
nothing detached or casual about this sort of
interchange. When what is being shared has
authenticated itself in the crucible of one's own
experience and is of vital necessity to the other,
this makes for a powerful transaction indeed.

A friend of mine joined the army back in
World War II and was immediately assigned to
an airborne division. This dismayed him no

little, for he was a country boy and had never so much as been up in an airplane, much less jumped out of one with a parachute! However, he was sent to a highly concentrated para-troopers' school, and he told me later that no one had to encourage him to pay attention to his instructor. He literally hung on every word that man was saying, for he realized in a matter of days he would be jumping out the door of a plane, and what he knew or did not know would be a matter of life and death. And, he reported, the fact that the instructor was himself a sea-soned paratrooper added validity to what he said. Here was a human being sharing with other human beings what he knew about a subject of vital concern. I would suggest that this provides a better description of what the preach-ing event ought to be than for some casual academic dilettante to pass out information that, even if correct, is of little existential moment. We are called to be and do far more than merely pass out information.

In fact, our task is summed up beautifully in the charge that was given to the unknown prophet of the Exile whose words are recorded in the document of Second Isaiah. The King James Version puts it this way: "Comfort ye, comfort ye my people, saith your God. Speak ye comfortably to Jerusalem" (Isa. 40:1). George Adam Smith translated that second phrase, "Speak home to the hearts of Jerusalem."[3] That really is what authentic preaching is supposed to be. It is penetrating the deepest levels of consciousness with concerns of ultimate import. And the most appropriate vehicle for this kind of interaction is the truth that has come home to us through our own honest grappling with life. What chance, really, does truth have of happening *through* us if first of all it has not happened *to* us? How can I really speak with existential urgency to you and your woundedness when I have not myself braved that struggle or come to know through the crucible of my own experience that this or that has saving power? It is for this reason, I think, that the great German theologian-preacher Helmut Thielicke has concluded that the two most powerful forms of preaching are what he calls "declaration" and "confession."[4] I take these to mean a willingness to share out of both my own light and my own darkness—to share the truths that are saving me and the places where I find the struggle still to be most acute. This dual form of preaching may well "speak home to the heart" of another and get past all those massive barriers that we humans erect against each other.

To engage in this kind of preaching means that I would do well not to traffic in lots of affirmations that may be true but have not yet become truth for me. I wish I had learned this lesson much earlier. I was raised in a hyper-evangelical religious atmosphere, and I experienced lots of pain by getting ahead of myself and attempting to witness to others about what I had never really received myself in an authentic way. I began my religious pilgrimage like all others, taking over from family and culture those beliefs that they found to be true. I was never encouraged "to ask and seek and knock" on my own. Rather we were taught the chorus "Only Believe."[5] This way of handling religious reality got me into lots of trouble in my earlier days.

For example, I remember precisely when my religious age of innocence came to an abrupt end. I was ten years old when a new family moved up the street from us in Nashville, Tennessee. The father had just retired from a career in the military. They had a son just about my age who turned out to be the most cosmopolitan peer I had ever encountered. He had lived in three different places overseas—the Panama Canal Zone, Germany, and the Philippines. He had actually been to places about which I had only read. I was utterly intrigued and stood somewhat in awe of this much-traveled lad.

One Sunday afternoon we were playing in my backyard and my mother called me to come in. My friend was obviously upset because our play was disrupted and asked why I had to leave. Without sensing that I was walking into a land mine, I answered, "I've got to go in and get dressed to go to church."

At the sound of that word, his face darkened and he said, "Church! Do you believe in that stuff? My father says that anybody who thinks there is a God is just a plain fool!"

I was absolutely flabbergasted at such a statement. My existence had been lived out in the protectiveness of the Bible Belt, and I had never heard words of this sort before. Here was a real live atheist in my own backyard! I was so frightened that I did what we humans usually do in panic—I struck back in anger at that which threatened me. The best defense is a good offense, I suppose, so I too got red in the face and said, "Well, my father believes there is a God. I think your father is the one who is a fool." And with that word of loving witness, I turned on my heels and went inside to get dressed to go to church and learn how to witness to the pagans!

However, something happened that afternoon which I was not able to dismiss from my mind, something you may find surprising for a child so young and so little trained in the philosophic arts. I remember lying awake on my bed that very night, with my mother listening to "The Old-fashioned Revival Hour" on the radio in the next room, sorting out the thing that had occurred. I remember saying to myself, "Here I am, believing that there is a God because my father says that there is one. And here is my friend, doing the same thing, only he is coming to the opposite conclusion." And then I was confronted by a question that I could not answer that night, namely, "How do you *know* that your father is right and his father is wrong?"

That incident marked the end of innocence for me as far as the whole question of religious certainty was concerned. It began to dawn on me that night that this is a big and diverse world, and that there are many fathers making many different affirmations about ultimate reality. There had to be a better reason for one's religious conclusions than the opinion of some other person. As of that night, I became a person with questions, acquainted with doubt, and I began a process of asking and seeking and knocking that was to take me in many directions and through all kinds of uncertainties.

Not long after this awakening in the backyard, the church I attended sponsored a youth revival, and a college student with more vitality than wisdom came to preach for a week. The pastor of our church was an utterly faithful and steadfast man, but there was not an ounce of excitement about him. Thus, by contrast, this brash young evangelist who wore loud clothes and carried a trombone into the pulpit was an absolute marvel to behold. His sheer physical activity in the pulpit was enough to rouse me out of the habits of inattention which I had already by that time developed.

One night he addressed himself to the subject of doubt, and told us how he had come to a place in his life when he was not sure about any of the ultimate questions. I really pricked up my ears and listened carefully as he told how the problem of doubt had been resolved in his own life. One night in his college dorm room, he had taken a copy of the Holy Bible, opened it on the floor, got down on his hands and knees before it—a stance which he proceeded to demonstrate right there before us in the pulpit—and said, "Holy Bible, I do not understand all your teachings. I cannot answer the many arguments that are leveled against you. But I hereby choose to believe that you are the Truth, that you are the Word of God. And I hereby will speak where you speak and be silent where you are silent. I hereby accept you unequivocally as Ultimate Truth." He had gotten up off his knees, he said, and never had a moment's doubt from that time forward.

Well, there I sat, ten years old, no longer living in the innocence of unbroken certainty, taking it all in. And the answer came in a flash. "Of course! Here is how I can know that my father is right and my friend's father is wrong. Here is a book that everyone accepts, a document of great antiquity and sacredness. Things are true because the Bible says they are true. This is the shape of religious authority."

I must confess that this was a giant leap forward in my own spiritual unfolding. Suddenly I felt as if I had ground under my feet, a reason for the faith within me. That set off a period of reading the Bible with great interest, of grounding faith in something as secure as the words you could point to on a given page. This particular form of religious authority served me well for several years, until I had another fateful encounter.

This time the person was an exchange student from Iran. He had come to Nashville under the auspices of the American Friends' Service Committee, but soon after he arrived, the family with whom he was to stay was transferred. The Friends' Committee worked out living arrangements with a family that had no children in our high school, and this left the student rather unattached. The principal asked me if I would take this foreigner under my wing and befriend him. It was the beginning of a very meaningful relationship—one that moved below the surface and got to where it touched many of the vital springs of existence.

One evening after I had eaten supper in the home where he was living and the two of us had gone up to his bedroom to visit, the question of religion came up for the first time. I remember asking him if he believed that Jesus was the Son of God who had come to die for our sins. In his characteristically polite way, he said, "No, why should I?" With that I reached for my Soul-winner's New Testament, and had every intention of pasting John 3:16 right on his forehead. But he raised his hand and said, "Wait a minute. I do not accept something as true just because it is written in the Holy Bible. As far as I am concerned, that is nothing but a book of myth and superstition. I do not accept it!"

I cannot tell you how astonished I was. Remember now, this was Nashville, Tennessee—*the* headquarters of Southern Evangelical Christianity—and I had never in all my life encountered a person who did not accept the authority of the Bible. Now, to be sure, I had known lots of people who did not take it very seriously, but I had never encountered *anyone* who said openly that he or she did not believe the Bible was true.

In that moment Amad turned the tables on me by asking, "Do you believe that Allah is the only true God and Mohammed is his prophet?" "No," I said, "why should I?" And then, so help me, he reached over on his bookshelf, brought out a volume that looked for all the world like the Holy Bible—it was black and morocco-bound—except that across the cover were the words *The Koran*, and he said, "Because this holy book says that this is true."

Now I was absolutely dumfounded. I had never even heard of such a document. But in that moment, the question that had first haunted my life at the ripe old age of ten returned, only this time it said, "How do you know that your book is right and his book is wrong?" There was no answer, and the situation got so awkward that I excused myself as quickly as I could and went stumbling out into the night.

The walk home that evening was long indeed. I could take you to the very street corner in Nashville where I stopped, looked up at the heavens, and said: "This religion business is a whole lot more complicated than I realized." At that point I began to plead, "Who are you anyway, God? Are you Jehovah? Are you Allah? Who are you? Will the true God please stand up?" And then I started to bargain: "If you will just give me a hint as to who you are, I will do my best to accept you, to build my life around you. I really want to know the truth. Mystery, Mystery, what is your name?"

If intensity alone is enough to justify a response, I should have gotten one that night, for no adolescent was ever any more in earnest than I was. But as I stood there pouring out my innermost heart, the heavens remained as silent as a tomb. There was no answer that night, or the next night, or the next week, or the next month, or the next year. I know from personal experience what is meant by "the silence of God," "the absence of God," yes, even "the death of God." I know what it is like to want more than anything else in the world to know God but not to have any evidence outside yourself on which to ground that certainty. I know what it is like to fall through space, to feel that nothing you touch stays put.

The events of that night marked the beginning of my most traumatic time of not knowing. I remember several things about it. After the initial times of pleading, it dawned on me that there probably was not going to be a quick resolution to this matter. I also remember coming to terms with the fact that I simply did not know for myself certain things about which other people seemed confident.

At the time, unfortunately, I was not a part of a religious community which understood the relation between doubt and faith. I remember gingerly trying to discuss this matter with a few of the adults who went to our church, but all I got was an avalanche of condemnation. When I asked my Sunday school teacher how one could know that the Bible was true and the Koran false, he turned red in the face and said: "The idea—your asking questions like that with the kind of mother you have!" Of course, this response had nothing to do with the nature of my quest. I did not need condemnation or exhortation. I needed evidence. But it was not available in the church of my adolescence. However, by what I take to be a miracle of grace, I did not turn bitter and cynical and decide that since I did not know, I could not know. I went underground, sensing that I could not really rely on the adults in that community, but believing that somehow, if I would open the windows of my life a full 360 degrees around me and keep on asking and seeking and knocking, perhaps, in time, I could discover a basis for certainty.

It was in that spirit that I went off to college, and there goodness and mercy followed me in a marvelously appropriate way. During my freshman year I encountered a religion professor fresh out of Yale Divinity School who had come back to teach at a little junior college in North Carolina called Mars Hill. Carl Harris was a bachelor, and he lived in the basement of the same dorm in which I was rooming. He took an interest in my doubt and patiently heard me out as I gradually unfolded it to him. Instead of condemning me for not believing, he kept saying, "You ought to look at this. You ought to read that." He responded to my questions with evidence, not condemnation.

That Christmas someone gave me a copy of J. B. Phillips's little book, *Your God Is Too Small.*[6] For some reason I did not open it until one warm spring afternoon, and then I was utterly intrigued by his argument. Phillips makes a real case for incarnational Christianity. Again and again he refers to the Gospel of John. To be honest, I had not worked with the Bible for some time, but that particular afternoon I put down the little volume by Phillips and picked up the

Bible. Turning to the beginning of John's Gospel, I started reading the prologue: "In the beginning was the Word, and the Word was with God, and the Word was God. . . . And the Word was made flesh and dwelt among us."

At this point I have trouble putting into words exactly what happened. It was as if I had been in the place of great silence and suddenly there came the sound of many waters; in a place of great darkness and suddenly a bright light began to shine; utterly alone and suddenly realized myself to be companioned by Another. There rose up around me the overwhelming feeling, "This is true. To the mystery of Godness the man Jesus does give a face. He is the clue to the Ultimate Reality."

This was not what I was expecting to learn that afternoon. In fact, to be honest, it was not even a conclusion I particularly wanted to be true at that time in my life. But here, suddenly, from beyond myself, Reality broke in and authenticated Itself. And I responded by saying simply, "Yes! Yes! I accept. I sit down before fact like a little child." As Gert Behanna puts it, "God happened to me" that afternoon.[7] He came in the form of an event, and for the first time in my life, to use Pascal's words, the heart had its reasons that reason knows not of.[8]

I realized then that faith is not believing in the unbelievable, nor is it committing intellectual suicide and taking a leap into the dark. But faith is response on our part to the inthrust of God. He and he alone is the ultimate basis here—not another person's opinion, even if it is one's own father; not a book, not an institution, but the Mystery of God himself authenticated through actual experience. This is why we are called to be *witnesses*, not soul winners, for all we can really do is relate, like a witness in a courtroom, our experience of the Almighty. He must do the rest. It is not our responsibility to go into the jury box and strong-arm others to accept our word. We let what has happened *to* us happen *through* us— that and only that.

This is what St. Paul did in his missionary activities. Someone asked me one time why the account of Paul's conversion appears three times in the Book of Acts. "Probably," I answered, "because he told it, not three times, but three thousand times. In fact, whenever he went to a new place, I imagine he began by saying, 'Let me tell you how I got into all this,' and then recounted his story." Such retelling is what Thielicke means by "declaration." I believe that it really does constitute the only thing we have to give positively to others. That which is saving me in my woundedness I offer to you—anything else is illegitimate.

Not only that, this methodology also corresponds to the particular shape of today's religious climate. Claxton Monroe, an Episcopal rector from Houston, has suggested that only a word of honest testimony has much chance to penetrate the skepticism of today's unbelievers.[9] He acknowledges that all the older forms of authority have no validity to today's secular skeptic. We have been trained scientifically to let evidence shape our conclusions, no matter how we may feel about it. Thus, Monroe says, a lay person who has no axe to grind or vested interest to serve may sometimes penetrate that defensive grid that so many people put up. I think he is correct. And even the ordained clergy, when he or she dares to make available the truth that has come home to them in honest grappling, can speak home to the hearts of otherwise unbelieving folk. The declarative form of preaching, then, is at once the only form of truth we have a right to share, and the form of truth that has the best chance of making contact in the skeptical age in which we live.

Declaration, however, is only one form of effective preaching, according to Thielicke. The other is "confession," that willingness to share, not out of our light, but out of our darkness and what we have experienced there. I am convinced that there is tremendous potency in this strategy, for it enables us to get at one of the most delicate challenges of the ministry, namely, how to be prophetic, how to deal with a sick situation in ways that will set in motion a process of healing rather than intensifying the difficulty.

I must confess that this strategy is something I did not get in my seminary training. I went out into the parish woefully ignorant of the dynamics of being a positive change-agent, and thus was counterproductive in many of my efforts. My strategy back then was to hit the issue head-on and call for change on the basis of condemnation. 'This is wrong," I would thunder, "and in the name of the Lord, I pronounce a curse on all of this until it is changed." Such pronouncements took enormous courage and boldness; the trouble was, they did not produce positive change at all. Like the shrine of Bethel in the wake of Amos's denunciations, if anything the situations became more rigid and more resistant to change than ever before.

But slowly it dawned on me that change of any kind is more complex and ambiguous than I had realized, even in my own life. To be sure, part of me wants change and responds positively to the possibility of growth and development. But other parts of me are frightened to death at the prospect. There is an element of gain and loss in every experience of change, and the fearful side of me magnifies the dimension of loss and says, "Bad as the present might be, at least I know what I am dealing with. Who knows what the changed situation will be like?"

So here we are, both attracted to and repulsed by the prospect of change. The challenge becomes how to mobilize the forces that want to change against the forces that oppose change? I learned in the early days of my parish ministry that condemnation is not effective for such a purpose. It feels like attack, whether it is meant to be that or not, and we humans instinctively defend ourselves in such situations. Thus, instead of mobilizing energy to move or change, condemnation does the very opposite. It makes one more defensive and provokes one to counterattack with "You're not so great yourself. Who made you a judge over me?"

I think this is precisely what Jesus meant in the passage when he says: "Judge not, that you be not judged" (Matt. 7:1, RSV). A better translation would be, "Condemn not." Jesus is talking here not about discernment but rather about the contempt that is vomited forth on a certain

condition. He goes on to use an Oriental hyper-
bole, the picture of a person with a two-by-four
stuck in his eye proposing to remove a speck of
sawdust from another's eye. No one in his right
mind would submit to an operation under those
conditions. So Jesus is saying that change called
for out of a stance of condemnation is counterproductive. It may make you feel better to
have gotten off your chest how bad you perceive
another to be, but in terms of doing anything
positive about the problem, matters are probably
worse than before. People rarely confess to their
critics. They are reluctant to show their broken
parts to someone they perceive as despising
them.

But in this same passage, Jesus suggests another alternative. If, instead of moving to take
the speck of sawdust out of another's eye, we
went to work on the two-by-four in our own eye,
all kinds of change might be set in motion. It is
true, people rarely confess to their critics, but
they do open up to a fellow struggler. If I begin
to grapple openly with the darkness that is in my
own life, that not only lifts a sense of shame
from others, it also injects hope into the situation. Another may begin to say: "If he is having
to struggle with such-and-such and feels that
something can be done about it, maybe I can

admit my struggle too and join him." People begin to come out of the woodwork from all directions when we start saying "we" about a certain problem instead of the angry "you." Suddenly there is companionship in the struggle and a new sense of hope.

I am here to report that more has happened redemptively when I have dared to preach confessionally than ever came of angry denunciation. When I stopped saying "you" and started saying "we" to the problems of racial prejudice or the war in Vietnam or poverty and all the rest, conflict and anguish were not eliminated, but the bitterness and the feeling of adversary versus adversary were removed. Suddenly we all seemed to be on the same level. My admitting that what another needed was what I needed too, moved us to stand together before Christ in the hope that he could do for me what he could do for the other. I do not want to sound simplistic and say that all the problems of history can be solved by confession alone. But for me, at least, admitting where the darkness touches me and how I am having to struggle with it has been a more fruitful means of producing change than the way of condemnation.

Not everyone will like this, of course. There are those who want the minister to present a façade of perfection and are offended when he or she acknowledges clay feet or the reality of a shadow-side in their lives. This happened to me when our ten-year-old daughter died of leukemia back in 1970. I did not attempt to preach for one month after she died, and this in itself bothered some who wanted me to bound right back into the pulpit with affirmations. When finally I was able to preach, I was quite honest about both the light and the darkness that had come to me in that situation. I acknowledged moments of anger and doubt and frustration with God as well as times of consolation and insight. After I had finished this sermon, some people were aghast at a preacher's saying right in the pulpit that he had doubts and uncertainties. Yes, there were those people. But the majority seemed to feel a new bond of kinship because of my confession. To this day I have contact with people who say, "I remember your admitting having to struggle with grief. I think you will understand my anguish."

Perhaps our greatest usefulness to each other is not in the relation of strength to weakness—the stance of a rescuer—but in that of weakness to weakness—the two of us in the darkness together, but for that reason no longer alone or without hope.

I come back, then, to my one suggestion in terms of the *how* of preaching. Let it be the fruits of our own woundedness made available to the woundedness of others. Declaration and confession—my light and my darkness—these are all we have to give, really. Only that which has happened to us can happen through us. If I would "speak home" to your heart and get through the defensive grid system you have erected, the two best gifts I have to give are the things that are saving me and the places where I am still struggling. As Simon Peter said to the beggar at the Gate Beautiful, "Silver and gold have I none; but such as I have, give I thee" (Acts 3:6, KJV). The only thing we have to share ultimately is our experience. To be willing to share that fully as "a wounded healer" is one of the secrets of great preaching.

5

The Preaching
Event:

When?

The Preacher as Nurturer

There is one last question I want to explore in relation to the preaching event, and that has to do with the issue of timeliness. I have used the words *what, why,* and *how* in previous attempts to understand more fully the process of preaching. The word for this last chapter is *when.* I want to examine what role the reality of time plays in the act of preaching.

One of the things that distinguishes biblical religion from other systems and philosophies is the fact that it does take history seriously. Both time and space are taken into account in the way the God Yahweh does his work. Now to be sure, they are by no means the only factors in his

111

economy, but they are significant to him. Take, for example, the Old Testament saga of Moses. Here was a man who was concerned about the plight of his native people from the very beginning of his life. You will remember that he had been born into a Hebrew family at a time of great persecution in Egypt, when the edict was out that all male Hebrew infants be killed at birth. Moses' mother was ingenious enough to devise a form of civil disobedience, and when this was detected by Pharaoh's own daughter, instead of indulging in recrimination, she had Moses adopted into the royal family and raised in the labyrinth of the Egyptian palace, where he grew up and was educated among the nobility.

It soon became apparent, however, that Moses was made of noble stuff. It has been said that there are really only two kinds of persons in history: those who want to make the world a better place for everyone, and those who simply want to make a better place for themselves in the world as it is. At this point, Moses clearly emerges in the former category. Instead of taking his incredible good fortune for granted and never looking back, he chose to be concerned with what was happening to the rest of his kinfolk who had not been as fortunate as he. That is to say, he could not enjoy the ease and comfort into which he had fallen while the rest of his people were languishing under oppression. In his early manhood, this concern came to expression in an act of impulsive violence.

One day Moses witnessed an Egyptian overlord mistreating a Hebrew, and—as is so typical of adolescent indignation—he proceeded to answer one injustice with another—that is, he killed the oppressor with his own bare hands. It is not clear what Moses hoped to accomplish by this act. Did he expect it "to speak to the blood" of his fellow Hebrews and become the spark that would ignite a national uprising? No one can say. All we know is that obviously the time was not right for such a revolution. The Hebrew people were not to that point of ferment in their own discontent, nor was the Egyptian establishment ripe for this sort of shift. The end result was that Moses had to flee for his life into the desert wastes of Midian, there to begin the life of a wandering fugitive.

Once again, it is a sign of Moses' character that he did not either blow up in anger or give up in despair over this turn of events. He took responsibility for the consequences that had resulted from his actions and settled into not just making the best of the situation, but making the most of the opportunities that were before him. He became a desert herdsman and for forty years tended sheep in that desolate terrain. In the process he learned the topography of that country like the back of his hand. He also cultivated the sensitivity that can be the legacy of the solitude of the desert, and honed his perceptive powers so that he could detect even a small signal from the Almighty.

Decades later, these uses to which he had put his life in the wilderness bore incredible fruit. His desert eye, sharpened by years of solitude, enabled him to notice something that a city-bred man might easily have missed, namely, a bush that was burning but not being consumed. Although he was well along in years by then, Moses had not lost the capacity for wonder. He still could be intrigued by that which he had never seen before. And so he turned aside to explore this unprecedented phenomenon, and there the voice of the Mystery spoke to him and made clear that the time was now right to fulfill the dream of his heart. At last the Hebrews were to a point in their discontent and the Egyptians at such a place of weakness that what he had dreamed of was now historically possible.

At this moment *the time was right!* The desire for liberation that burned in Moses' spirit had a timeless quality about it, but the possibility of enacting it had to wait for the appropriate moment. This is what I mean about biblical religion taking time and space seriously. All things are not possible at any given moment. "There is a tide in the affairs of men," says Shakespeare, which must be noted if certain things are going to be. St. Paul had the same understanding when he wrote to the Galatians that "in the fulness of time, God sent forth his Son, born of woman, born under the Law" (4:4). There were conditions existing at the moment Jesus of Nazareth stepped on the stage of history that had never existed before and would never exist again in that particular combination. Thanks to the Roman Empire there was political peace around the Mediterranean Basin, there people spoke a common language, and there was a ferment of discontent and expectation in the religious realm that was precisely right for the Christ event.

There are teachable moments and appropriate occasions when things are possible that could never have been before and never could be again. This is a factor that the Christian preacher must take into account if he wants to speak home to the hearts of his hearers in a way that can effectively help reestablish a relation of trust between them and their Creator. Other considerations are certainly important as well, but if the question of timeliness is ignored, the effectiveness of the whole process can be disrupted.

I find this vision of reality to be utterly authentic. It has to struggle to stay alive, however, because so much in us wants to do away with the dimension of timeliness and tries to reduce all of life to timeless rules and formulas that can be applied no matter what the particular situation. We humans are bipolar creatures by nature. We have a side that longs for security as well as a side that is hungry for adventure and movement and creativity. The challenge in life is to find a vital balance between these two polar needs. However, our security need—that hunger for order and certainty and the elimination of all risk—prompts us to want to find certain unchanging laws that are true no matter what the historical context. In my judgment, this is what the right-wing conservatives are intent on doing.

Down in my part of the country, a man named Bill Gothard can fill a coliseum with twelve thousand people for thirty hours of monological instruction in one week's time. When you analyze the secret of this approach, it comes down to a timeless form of legalism. No Jesuit seminary of old ever prescribed a pattern of behavior more minutely than does Gothard in one of his Institutes on Basic Youth Conflicts. Here is a "Yellow Pages" approach to life if there ever was one, which leaves out the element of timeliness altogether. All you have to do in any given situation is locate the appropriate prescription.

Although Gothard cites a specific scriptural reference for all his rules, in my judgment he misses the whole spirit of the biblical vision. Scripture tells us that nothing is bad in itself, just as no one note of a piano is "bad" in and of itself. It all depends on how a thing is used, how a note is tuned and played. My professor of ethics in the seminary used to say that "everything bad was something good misused." He dared us to identify any particle of creation that was always and everywhere bad. Take water, for example. It can do horrible things—destroy priceless paintings or stifle human life if a face is held under it long enough. But that same substance can also quench our thirst and wash our bodies and float us from one place to another. In and of itself, water is neither good nor bad. Its goodness or badness depends on how it is used in relation to its original design. Which means that the question of timeliness and appropriateness is absolutely foundational. There is no one thing that is always right or wrong irrespective of particular circumstances. Should one human being take a knife and cut open another human being? For a mugger in the act of stealing or raping, the act has one character to it. For a surgeon in the act of removing an inflamed appendix, the act has an altogether different meaning.

My point in dwelling on this matter is that we humans do have to improvise, it seems to me, to live authentically in our kind of world. The desire to eliminate the need for discernment and decision-making in a particular context is, in my judgment, a refusal to be who we really are as human creatures. There are no timeless laws or formulas that can be applied automatically or without consideration of the particular situation. Like it or not, matters of timing and appropriateness are utterly crucial in life, and to leave them out in the practice of the preaching art would be disastrous indeed.

I once heard George Kelsey, the great black ethicist at Drew University, say that he learned from his boyhood experience on a farm in Tennessee that there were three distinct stages of development in growing a crop. First the plants were green, then they were ripe, then they were rotten, and to participate meaningfully in the farming process meant to take these stages seriously and know what to do when. I think this applies to the work of the preacher as well. That is why I have chosen the term *nurturer* to describe this aspect of the preaching task. The image is drawn from the realm of agriculture and suggests that one who works with growing things must understand the successive stages of their pattern of development and cultivate a sense of timing as to what is appropriate to do when.

What, then, is the preacher as nurturer to do? I have several suggestions.

The first thing preachers must do is to acquaint themselves with the general contour of the human saga, to learn what is involved functionally in floating down the stream of personhood—infancy, childhood, adolescence, young adulthood, middle adulthood, and finally, old age. While there is enormous diversity in each individual's experience, at the same time there is commonality as well, certain predictable growth challenges that occur for all persons. Thus, it is essential that the preacher as timely nurturer saturate himself or herself in this knowledge as thoroughly as possible.

We are very fortunate that just now so much is being done in all the disciplines to illumine a stage of life long neglected, namely, adulthood. Back in 1931, Carl Jung wrote that the afternoon of life is radically different from morning and has to be coped with in a different fashion. "But where," he asked, "are the universities to prepare us for this stage of our lives?"[1] Almost all of our formal education focuses on the tasks of the morning of life. Think about it. What are the issues dealt with in elementary, secondary, and college education? The primary focus here is on the beginning tasks of life—leaving one's family origins, establishing an individual identity, arriving at one's own hierarchy of values, deciding on a career, selecting a mate. But what about that forty- to fifty-year period that stretches from the time you get out of school and settle into coping with the everydayness of every day? The kinds of attention paid to infancy, early childhood, and adolescence have not been paid to this era. But now, thanks to the work of persons like Daniel Levinson of Yale and popularizers like Gail Sheehy, that balance is being redressed. They are enabling us to see what happens in the twenties, thirties, forties and fifties is not as mysterious or dismaying as we may have once thought. There are predictable shifts in feelings and perceptions, and to know about them ahead of time is helpful indeed. I can see nothing but good resulting from this increase in knowledge, for here as everywhere, what we do not know most assuredly does hurt us. The things I simply happen upon in life for which I have no preparation can be so frightening and bewildering that my chances of negotiating them positively are greatly diminished. Ignorance is never bliss— certainly not with something as awesome as the many shapes of the mid-life crisis.

One of the good things that I got out of my ministry in Texas was a delightful story about a certain Mexican bank robber by the name of Jorge Rodriguez, who operated along the Texas border around the turn of the century. He was so successful in his forays that the Texas Rangers put a whole extra posse along the Rio Grande to try and stop him. Sure enough, late one afternoon, one of these special Rangers saw Jorge stealthily slipping across the river, and trailed him at a discreet distance as he returned to his home village. He watched as Jorge mingled with the people in the square around the town well and then went into his favorite cantina to relax. The Ranger slipped in and managed to get the drop on Jorge. With a pistol to his head he said, "I know who you are, Jorge Rodriguez, and I have come to get back all the money that you have stolen from the banks in Texas. Unless you give it to me, I am going to blow your brains out." There was one fatal difficulty, however. Jorge did not speak English and the Texas Ranger was not versed in Spanish. There they were, two adults at an utter verbal impasse.

But about that time an enterprising little Mexican came up and said, "I am bilingual. Do you want me to act as translator?" The Ranger nodded, and he proceeded to put the words of the Ranger into terms that Jorge could understand. Nervously, Jorge answered back: "Tell the big Texas Ranger that I have not spent a cent of the money. If he will go to the town well, face north, count down five stones, he will find a loose one there. Pull it out and all the money is behind there. Please tell him quickly." The little translator got a solemn look on his face and said to the Ranger in perfect English, "Jorge Rodriguez is a brave man. He says he is ready to die."

As Jorge found out, what we do not know most assuredly does hurt us. If only Jorge had studied English! If only the Ranger had been versed in Spanish! Today we are in a much better position than Jorge, as far as knowledge of human growth is concerned. Light is now being made available from many sources on the contour of the whole human saga. The preacher who would fulfill the role of timely nurturer has a sacred obligation to learn as much as he or she can and utilize it in deciding what to do and when, so that other people's growth may be helped.

The second thing preachers must do is learn how to listen carefully and perceptively. My great mentor in the ministry, Carlyle Marney, who was to have given these lectures in 1980, was fond of saying that if we listen to our people for twenty hours a week, then we have a right to speak for twenty minutes on Sunday morning. A person may want to quarrel with Marney about his numbers, but I do not think we can quarrel with the organic relationship between listening and preaching appropriately. If we do not go to the trouble of perceiving where our people are—the questions they are asking, the point where they are in their own struggling—then it will be virtually impossible to speak a relevant and appropriate word to their situations.

Paul Tillich's famous method of correlation, in which he suggested that we let culture define the questions and revelation provide the answers is a fine working model for authentic preaching. But the crucial ingredients that make such a process functionally effective are the willingness and the ability to listen—first of all to perceive where another person is so that one then has some inkling of what aspect of the revelation corresponds to their need. However, none of us should think that something that sounds as familiar as listening is thereby easy or automatic. Do you have any realization of how difficult it is really and truly to hear another person; that is, to so empty yourself of past experiences and all the passions and prejudices that make up your present reality that you really do create enough space where another can be himself and herself on their own terms?

Somewhere in his writings Søren Kierkegaard[2] tells about a small circus that traveled from little town to little town in his native Denmark. The pattern of the troupe was to come into a community, hand out announcements of their performance, and then put up a tent on the outskirts of the village for that evening. On one particular occasion, the circus tent caught fire about an hour before the performance was to start. It turned out that the clown was the only member of the troupe who was fully dressed, and so he was dispatched into the village to get help as quickly as he could. The clown discharged his responsibility perfectly. He apprised everyone he met of the crisis and begged them to get their water pails and come out to help. However, the people in this village had had prior experiences with clowns. They had built up in their minds certain expectations about these folk. So, according to Kierkegaard, *they heard the clown with their eyes;* that is, they assumed that he was on a mission of entertainment and that this was just a new way of drumming up a crowd. Not until they looked on the horizon and saw the ominous red glow did it dawn on them that in this moment what they were encountering was not a clown at all, but a human being dressed in a clown's costume bearing an urgent and utterly real message!

I think of this story often as I ponder the whole process of speaking and listening, of one human being saying something to another. If we are not careful, the experiences we have had in the past with a certain individual or with people of whom that individual reminds us become the reality with which we interact. It is as though I painted the windows of my house with certain images of my own choosing; from then on, what I do business with through those windows is not the outside world at all, but figments of my own making. This is what the word *stereotype* is all about—a picture in the head we so easily allow to grow and block off interaction with the new and the real. It is hard to keep the past in its place and not allow it to contaminate our present experience.

In this connection, it occurs to me that there may be a deep inner relation between two statements of Jesus which are repeated again and again in the Gospel records. I am referring to his dictum, "If anyone would come after me, let him deny himself, take up his cross, and follow me," and the words, "He that hath ears to hear, let him hear." There is a real act of self-denial in every authentic experience of hearing. I am called to turn down the record that is forever playing in my head so that there is silence enough for me to hear a word from beyond. It is so easy for me to project upon another a shadow out of my own past experience rather than letting that person be what he or she is in this moment, and receive in that moment a new and fresh experience. This is the true meaning of hospitality, a quality held in the highest regard in the Old Testament. Henri Nouwen describes it as "creating an open space where strangers can cast off their strangeness," and give to us the distinctive gifts which are theirs.[3]

One of the keys, then, of being a timely nurturer is to develop the art of listening in all its profundity. It is by no means an easy thing to do, but it is absolutely crucial if our preaching is to be an authentic meeting of realities, not just a soliloquy with our own preconceived images. Whoever would speak the timely and appropriate word must learn how to listen, and then must make of that listening the beginning point in the shaping of the word.

It is clear to me that part of Jesus' incredible power was the appropriateness of his words to the place where the individuals before him found themselves. Take, for example, his celebrated encounter with the woman at the well of Sychar. That conversation was revolutionary in many ways.

This particular human being was shocked that a Jewish male, and a religious leader at that, would have chosen to engage in conversation with her in any form, much less in the kind and depth of conversation he initiated. But this is part of the remarkable revolution that Jesus of Nazareth began. He took words that for centuries had functioned as nouns—words like *male* and *female, Jew* and *Gentile, Samaritan, rich, poor, good, bad*—and reduced them to the level of adjectives. That is, what had once been definitive categories—when you said that about a human being, you said everything there was to say—Jesus deemphasized into descriptive modifiers that merely pointed to certain aspects of a person. He took the descriptions *person* and *human being* and elevated those to the nominative category. This is the revolution St. Paul was referring to when he wrote to the churches in Galatia: "In Christ, there is neither Jew nor Greek, there is neither bond nor free, there is neither male nor female, but ye are all one in Him (3:28, KJV). It is a revolution that we are still trying to catch up with twenty centuries later. So the very fact that Jesus would take the initiative and speak to the woman at the well—female, Samaritan, prostitute—and give to her what he would have given to any male or Jew, and expect of her what he would have expected of any man or Jew or righteous person—that is one astonishing thing about this encounter.

But what amazed the woman even more, it seems, was not just what he said, but that he really listened to her. Here was a woman who had been intimate with many across the years, but had never been really close to a single person. Here was a person who had been loved after a fashion again and again, and yet at another level had never really felt herself loved or esteemed in a profound way. Thus, the experience with this One by Jacob's Well was absolutely overwhelming. She who had come out at noon to avoid the angry stares of the other women now dropped all of her shame and reticence and ran back into the village saying, "There is a man out there who told me every-thing I ever did." Or to translate it more deeply: "A man who really listened to me and spoke to my situation as no one else ever did."

And because there is so much hunger in all of us for the love that will listen and respond, the Fourth Gospel says that the whole village came running out to see this miracle for themselves. I have an idea this may have been the basis of Jesus' saying, "Look, the fields are white unto harvest." Back then, as they do even today, the folk who live in Palestine wear long white robes to protect themselves from the heat, and when they run, these robes stream out behind them. Thus, as these excited Samaritans came running from the village to the well, they must have made the whole hillside look white! In all of us there really is a deep hunger to be esteemed and listened to and taken seriously in our own individuality. Relating to folk the way Jesus did to this outcast woman is the high calling of the preacher who would be nurturer.

But there is one other suggestion I would make at this point. Having learned the topogra-phy of the human saga and found out through listening where other individuals are, the preacher as nurturer must know how to help them grow. We must know not only what blocks the flow of vitality but what will remove the blocks and get people moving forward again. I have found that thinking in terms of process and developmental growth is the most helpful frame of reference to apply here. This means that sin is regarded as incompleteness, a state of not-yet-what-it-could-be, rather than total corruption. Such a perspective opens the way for one to be utterly realistic about a given situation and at the same time hopeful. In my opinion, if either realism or hope is absent in a problem situation, the possibilities of creative progress are virtually nil.

Back in the 1960s, John Gardner observed that every institution in our society was caught in the brutal cross fire between uncritical lovers and unloving critics. I think he was correct in this assessment and in his feeling that either stance is an absolutely lethal situation for any living thing. Uncritical lovers are those who cannot bring themselves to acknowledge the presence of any kind of shadow in what they love, so they retreat into denial and belligerent fantasy that only leads into deeper and deeper darkness. On the other hand, unloving critics have no hope for what they see. They respond to imperfection with contempt and condemnation. And as I indicated earlier, condemnation simply stampedes those under attack into all kinds of defensiveness. I have found that setting a perspective of growth and process around all persons and situations alleviates the need to go to either of these extremes, and regarding imperfection as incompleteness makes it possible to be both realistic and hopeful. What neither the uncritical lover nor the unloving critic can do with the-less-than-perfect, the person who chooses the perspective of process and growth can do with zest.

It seems to me that this is consistent with the deepest and finest note of the Christian Gospel. Jesus came saying in effect, "You do not have to become perfect in order to get God to love you. God already loves you out of what he is, and his love becomes the dynamism of your becoming perfect." If God's love is the effect and our cleaning ourselves up and making ourselves perfect is the cause, what hope is there for any of us? But to hear that the love of God is gift and not wage, that in the Incarnation God has found a way to meet us where we are and to communicate with us as we are—that is an altogether different kind of process. Then both realism about our past and present *and* hope for the future become a possibility. Yet how hard it seems for us to unlearn and relearn this most basic of all sequences in our existence.

During my seminary days in Kentucky, I drove each weekend to a country church to serve a congregation of about a hundred souls. I had had very little pastoral experience before accepting this assignment, and so the first time I was to celebrate Holy Communion, I worked very hard to master the techniques and learn what to say when. As the Supper unfolded, I was dismayed to see that only six people out of a congregation of some seventy-five partook of either the loaf or the cup. I immediately concluded that I must have offended them in some way, saying the words of institution improperly or something. As soon as the benediction was pronounced, I asked the chairman of the deacons fearfully what had gone wrong. To my great dismay, I learned that what I had just witnessed was a longstanding tradition in that community. The word was out that to partake of the elements of the Lord's Supper was to imply that you considered yourself worthy, that you were living an exemplary Christian life and were thus celebrating your victory.

I spent the rest of my ministry at that church trying to counter that idea which is so utterly

The Preacher as Nurturer / 133

antithetical to the gospel. I did everything I could to show them that being perfect is not the way to get God to love us, that God's love of us is the secret of our becoming perfect, full grown, mature. The elements at the Lord's Table are much more like "the medicine of immortality," as the ancient church fathers put it, than they are champagne at a victory celebration. We do not partake of Christ's body and blood because we have earned the right to do so by our dazzling performance. We come there as patients who go to a hospital because they are sick, or people who go to a table because they are hungry. We partake of those sacraments because of our need, not our worthiness. The love of God is the power that makes perfection possible. It is not that which awaits perfection before it is given. I only hope I made some progress in correcting this longstanding misconception. At least, by the time I left, the number who participated had increased.

Communicating this understanding of the relation of God's love to our struggle and growth is utterly crucial in the preacher's task as nurturer. It embodies the whole difference between law and grace. The law condemns. The law demands. The law threatens and drives. And as St. Paul testifies so eloquently, the law triggers the rebel in us all (see Rom. 7:7–13). To be told I must do something or else I will not be loved, or that I shall be condemned if I do or do not do certain things, often makes me less disposed to act in the desired way. But if I am effectively told that there is nothing I can ever do that will make God love me any more than he loves me this moment, that there is nothing I can ever do that will make him stop loving me, then enormous powers of motivation are released in me, and "the perfect love that casteth out fear" begins to blow like wind in a sail to move me forward.

I am still waiting for a contemporary translation of the Gospels to convey this understanding in a passage which I fear has been the occasion for much neurotic perfectionism. I am referring now to the last verse of Matthew 5, where the King James Version has Jesus saying: "Be ye therefore perfect, even as your Father which is in heaven is perfect." Students of the Greek language know that this word *perfect* really means full-grown, complete, actualizing all of one's potential. They also know that the same verb form in Greek can be translated as either second person future indicative or as an imperative. I honestly think a better rendition of the sense of that passage would be, "You will be perfect, even as your Father in heaven is perfect, full-grown, complete." In other words, we have here the promise of what can come to be if grace is regarded as cause and not effect. Instead of saying, "First you become perfect and then you will be loved," the sense is, "You are loved, not because of what you have done, but because of what God is in his deepest nature. So if you will let him have his way, if you will allow him to collaborate with you, as he delights to do, the goal of it all will be your becoming perfect, full-grown, complete. All that he ever dreamed that you could be you will be. He will bring this to pass if you will let him." That is real security, real promise, real hope. When you realize that God's way always is process—first the seed, then the blade, then the flower—you have reason to be at once realistic about the way things are and at the same time hopeful as to what they can yet become. God is not finished with anything yet, nor is he a stranger to chaos or incompleteness. To get this word across to less than perfect people in appropriate and relevant ways would be the finest single thing the preacher could do as nurturer.

Which brings us back to where this journey started several pages ago—to preaching as event and to the preacher as reconciler, gift-giver, witness, and nurturer. What is it we are attempting to do when we stand up to preach? We are trying to participate in the restoring of a relation of trust between human creatures and the Creator. Why do we do this? Not to get something for ourselves, out of need-love, but to give something of ourselves in gift-love. How do we do it? By making available as witnesses what we have learned from our own woundedness for the woundedness of others. When do we do this? At times and in ways that are appropriate to another's growing as a farmer nurtures a crop. To do this is to participate in the extension of the gospel into our own time. Could anything be a higher human joy? I think not!

Let us go, then, under the mercy, with the great story, and in abundant hope. Amen.

Notes

Introduction
1. Quoted from Charles Williams in Sheldon Vanauken, *A Severe Mercy* (San Francisco & New York: Harper & Row, 1977), p. 119.

Chapter 1
1. Anonymous, "Words."

Chapter 2
1. Carl Sandburg, *Abraham Lincoln: The Prairie Years* (New York: Dell Publishing Co., 1954), 1:299.
2. P. T. Forsyth, *Positive Preaching and the Modern Mind* (London: Independent Press, 1907), p. 2.

Chapter 3
1. C. S. Lewis, *The Four Loves* (New York: Harcourt Brace, 1961).

2. Karen Horney, *Neurosis and Human Growth* (New York: W. W. Norton, 1950), p. 18.

3. Harry Emerson Fosdick, *A Book of Public Prayers* (New York: Harper & Bros., 1959).

4. Quoted by Martin E. Marty, "Reflections on the Congress of the Laity," *The Christian Century*, March 22, 1978, p. 194.

5. Arthur Miller, *Death of a Salesman* (New York: Viking Press, 1949).

6. Daniel J. Levinson, et al., *The Seasons of a Man's Life* (New York: Alfred A. Knopf, 1978); Gail Sheehy, *Passages* (New York: E. P. Dutton, 1976).

7. Miguel Unamuno, *The Tragic Sense of Life*, quoted by Carlyle Marney on a tape.

Chapter 4

1. Henri Nouwen, *The Wounded Healer: Ministry in Contemporary Society* (New York: Doubleday, 1972).

2. I heard Lloyd Ogilvie say this at the Summer Institute of Theology at Princeton Seminary, summer 1974.

3. George Adam Smith, *The Book of Isaiah* (New York: Harper & Bros., 1927), 2:76.

4. Helmut Thielicke, *Encounter with Spurgeon*, trans. John W. Doberstein (Philadelphia: Fortress Press, 1963).

5. Paul Rader, "Only Believe."

6. J. B. Phillips, *Your God Is Too Small* (New York: Macmillan, 1957).

7. Gert Behanna, in a spoken testimony.

8. Blaise Pascal, *Pensées*, #277 in Everyman edition (New York: E. P. Dutton), p. 78.

9. Claxton Monroe and William S. Taegel, *Witnessing Laymen Make Living Churches* (Waco, TX: Word Books, 1968).

Chapter 5

1. Carl Jung, *Modern Man in Search of a Soul*, trans. W. S. Dell and Cary F. Baynes (New York: Harcourt, Brace, 1955), pp. 108–9.

2. Søren Kierkegaard, *Either/Or*, 2 vols., trans. Walter Lowrie (Princeton: University Press, 1951).

3. Henri Nouwen, *Reaching Out: The Three Movements of Spiritual Life* (New York: Doubleday, 1975), chap. 5, "The Forms of Hospitality."